The African Ark

Bushbuck, drawn by John Prickett and reproduced
from *The Living Forest* by R. J. Prickett

R. J. Prickett

The African Ark

with 7 colour plates and
35 other illustrations by Frank W. Lane

David & Charles
Newton Abbot

0 7153 6258 5

Set in 11 on 13 pt Imprint
and printed in Great Britain
by Latimer Trend & Company Ltd Plymouth
for David & Charles (Holdings) Limited
South Devon House Newton Abbot Devon

TO JOHN

Contents

List of Plates

BLACK AND WHITE PLATES

COLOUR PLATES

Photographs taken in Kenya of wild and uncontrolled animals except the following:
Plates on pages 74, 76, 130–1, 151, 152 (top) (The Orphanage, Nairobi National Park); 75 (London Zoo); 152 (bottom) (Ngorongoro Crater); 73 (top) and 149 (bottom) were taken by R. J. Prickett, and that on page 149 (top) by John Karmali.

Foreword

Kenya today has one of the finest systems of National Parks in the world. Under the wise leadership of its president, the country has increased its total area from 9,486 square miles at the time of Independence to 10,078 square miles at the end of 1972. In addition to this vast area there is a further 1,646 square miles of protected area in the form of reserves such as those of the African District Councils and Forest Department.

The pressure on land for agricultural and industrial purposes is rising continuously and only proof of the value of wildlife can save it. Fortunately Kenya has a stable government and, because of this, tourism is an ever increasing source of revenue, besides being an extensive job-creative industry. Today it is second only to agriculture. Tomorrow it may be in the lead. During 1972 nearly 400,000 visitors came to Kenya. By far the primary attraction was game.

For very many years the forests of Kenya were a closed book to all except forest officers, game officers, and those few intrepid hunters who preferred facing the dangerous game there rather than in the more open thorn-bush. In their remote depths dwelt animals rarely seen . . . bongo, forest-hog, red duiker and suni.

The Ark game-viewing lodge was the first to be built deep within the forests of a National Park and in the habitat of those four rare and extremely shy animals. Others will doubtless follow and, just as the biblical Ark saved the animals from the rising floods, so will this newest and most modern Ark save the wild creatures from the rising destruction in the world today brought about by the thoughtless actions of man.

In this book Mr Prickett has described the animals, birds and trees of the forest; the building of The Ark to save them; their behaviour during the following three years, and finally, in a more humorous fashion, the behaviour of the visitors. Mr Lane has captured the wild beauty of the animals and their habitat in numerous photographs.

Just as The Ark has united beneath its roof people from all over the world, I hope and pray that this book will give them all a better understanding of this very beautiful country of ours . . . the Republic of Kenya.

Jan Mohamed, MP
Assistant Minister for Tourism and Wildlife
Republic of Kenya

Acknowledgements

I am indebted to the Honourable Jan Mohamed, Assistant Minister for Tourism and Wildlife of the Republic of Kenya, for so kindly writing the Foreword to this book.

I am also grateful to the following: Bill Woodley, Warden of the Kenya Mountain National Parks, who not only drew me the details of the sketch map of the Aberdares and Mount Kenya Parks, but made available his vast knowledge of those two mountains and placed the services of his staff at my disposal; Robin Higgin, Chairman of The Ark Ltd, who so kindly read the chapter 'The Ark Is Built'; Mogens Soeborg, Managing Director of The Ark Ltd, who told me how it was built and launched; and Kevin Lyons, late owner of The Country Club, then known as 'Steep', one of the directors of the company who told me about his dreams of a lodge deep in the forest and how those dreams came true.

I would also like to thank my wife, Gertrude Annie, for her encouragement and patience in enduring the endless noise of three typings of this book—with one finger. Also Mark Warwick who read my earliest draft and corrected a few biological details.

I am grateful to all the staff of The Ark Ltd, both those in the field and in Nairobi Head Office and also the booking agents, Percival Tours.

I have described at length in my chapter 'Human Behaviour inside The Ark' the pioneer work of the Hostesses Doreen Butterworth, Beverly Wood, Anna Bell and Vena Johansson. I would like here to express my appreciation of others, namely

Cecilia Kahiga, Ruth Woodley, Ali Evans, Kay Grieves Cook and Margaret Smith. They helped in many ways, especially when Frank was engaged on his photographic marathon of fifteen days and nights in The Ark. Also I would like to thank the Hunter, Ian Hardy.

Finally, this book could not have been published without the untiring help of my literary agent and photographer, Frank W. Lane.

Introduction

When I was asked to write a book on African wildlife based on my experiences, I felt at first that this would be quite impossible. I have been the privileged friend of some of the really great ones, men who have dedicated their whole lives to wildlife. In their company I still feel very humble.

My first experience with African wildlife was as a soldier in the East African campaigns of World War II, and for nearly five years it was destructive. War *is* destructive and in it wildlife is never spared. Then followed more than twenty years as a Forester, when I learned the meaning of conservation and was made Honorary Game Warden, a post I held for ten years.

Following my premature retirement in the cause of Africanisation in 1968, I worked for the National Parks, became a Professional Hunter, then became a Guide at the forest lodges of both Treetops and Secret Valley. When The Ark opened at the end of 1969 I joined the new company known as The Ark Ltd and have been with them ever since.

I suppose all this, over more than three decades, has given me more than my fair share of a way of life surpassed by none. Sometimes I feel a great sense of gratitude, and also a great sadness for those embroiled in the rat race of this present century.

We change as we grow older. Indeed, the story of evolution has been that the survival of the fittest has included those who were able to adapt themselves to a changing world. I once fought under the Union Jack. Had anybody at that time told me that one day I would change my allegiance then I would have said they were crazy. Amongst the host of reasons for doing this was the fact that Africa is the last great stronghold of the wild and these animals are in very real danger of ultimate extinction. To have deserted them would have constituted a grave betrayal. My duties have demanded that some should die. By my life's work many more have lived. If this book means that still more live then those I had to kill will not have died in vain.

Nyeri, Kenya   R. J. Prickett

Page 17 (*above*) Dick Prickett with a young Defassa waterbuck which had been caught by farm dogs but was rescued in time, taken on the lawn of Mrs Anne Jones; (*below*) view of The Ark from top of glade showing suspicious buffalo herd and three elephants outside the dungeon

Page 18 With snow-capped Mt Kilimanjaro as a backdrop, an elephant in the Amboseli Game Reserve placidly puffs dust over itself to get rid of insects

CHAPTER ONE

Hunting and the Role of
National Parks

A lot has been written about hunting in East Africa, much of it ill-informed. 'Game', as a Warden friend would say, 'is an emotional issue; when talking about it people lose all sense of proportion.' They forget that, according to scientists, man has been a hunter for millions of years. It is illogical to assume, as so many do, that he can stop and all will still be well. By hunting he has played a vital role in the delicate balance of nature, and its sudden withdrawal will inevitably lead to a decline in the ultimate fitness of the animals hunted. The true conservationist is not interested so much in the survival of a single animal as in the species as a whole.

When animal populations are in excess of the carrying capacity of their habitat, it is essential that the number be reduced. Whether the predator be man, beast or bird is immaterial. Yet there are people who state glibly that an animal has the right to live. An animal has only the right to be free and the right to die without unnecessary suffering.

The game laws of Kenya are as strict as any in the world. They have to be in a country containing such a wide variety of species, many of them dangerous. All visitors on a safari, whether to hunt or merely to photograph, must be accompanied by a qualified professional hunter. The country is divided into eighty-seven different hunting blocks or areas. The professional hunter must not only know their boundaries, but also what species of animals they contain and whether they are protected by law. In some places only photography is allowed. In one frontier area no vehicle is permitted and all safaris must be on foot or on camels.

Today a hunter is very restricted in the number of animals he may shoot. He must also never shoot within 200yd of his vehicle or within 500yd of a road. No shooting is allowed after dusk. There are special laws regarding female and juvenile animals. Certain animals are completely protected. Rifles also come under special laws: dangerous game must not be hunted with anything less powerful than a 0·375 magnum rifle. It is a serious offence not to follow up wounded animals. If the animal is one of the 'big five', failure to report the wounding may result in a prison sentence. If a hunter wounds and loses an animal it counts against his licence.

These very essential restrictions mean that, although hunting brings in a tremendous amount of revenue, both directly and indirectly, to a country which is by no means rich, it accounts for less than 1 per cent of the total animal population. Even this rarely effects the breeding capacity of the herds. The trophy animal usually attains his maximum horn growth *after* he leaves the herd and lives a solitary or bachelor herd existence.

In theory the Game Warden closes a hunting block whenever he finds that numbers of game are below what they should be. In practice he finds that poachers have taken advantage of the absence of safari parties and that, when reopened, there are fewer animals there than before. Yet, until a country can provide an alternative living for its hunting tribes it is quite unrealistic to expect them to refrain from following the way of life of their ancestors and starve.

In Kenya all the Wanderobo, the little hunters of the forest, are now settled in reserves. The Wakamba, the hunters of the plains and the bush-country, are now well established in farming. They are also often to be found in the army and administration, in trading, and in their wood-carving industry. The Wakikuyu are agriculturists; the Masai and the Nandi are pastorals. The Luo are traditional fishermen. So it is with many other lesser-known tribes. To a large extent therefore Kenya has now reached the stage where her people no longer must hunt in order to live.

In a National Park, of course, game is protected and hunting forbidden. Not only is no shooting allowed, but no human habitation may be built and activities such as cattle grazing or fire-wood collecting are also banned. Reserves, which operate along the same lines, may be National or belong to District Councils and have their own laws.

The need to protect game from uncontrolled hunting was realised by the British Administration in Kenya early in the present century. Apart from the establishment of the great Northern and Southern Game Reserves, little was done, however, until 1933, when Colonel Mervyn Cowie, later to become the first director of the National Parks, started campaigning for their formation against a wall of opposition. This came especially from farmers who lost a large amount of crops and stock to game without any compensation.

Colonel Cowie decided the only way to draw people's attention to the plight of these hunted animals was to jump on the bandwaggon and wildly advocate total destruction of all game whenever possible. Under a nom-de-plume, therefore, he wrote bloodthirsty letters to the *East African Standard*. At first the farmers were delighted. Here was a settler after their own hearts. A man who could stand up and tell the government just what to do with bloody game robbing them of their hard-earned money. But gradually it dawned on many people that Africa without its game would not be Africa. Not only would it not be Africa but it would not be a country worth living in.

So the tide of opinion began to flow in the opposite direction. It grew and grew until, in 1946, the government finally began to take notice and the area of Reserve outside Nairobi was gazetted as National Park.

Colonel Cowie was not only an ardent conservationist but also a capable administrator, and under him the Parks and Reserves grew in number until, at Independence, Kenya had without doubt, one of the finest National Park organisations in the world. Private donations were, and still are, the backbone of the structure but the government helps by giving grants on a proportionate basis. Today tourism is the second largest source of revenue, and is fast overtaking agriculture. It is the *game* that people come to see. In the near future it is planned that the National Parks and the Game Department will become one under the central government.

At 44 square miles Nairobi National Park is the smallest in the country, devoted solely to the preservation of mammals. Today Kenya has a marine park at the coast and others are being expanded or created continually. Nairobi National Park is unique in that its main gate is only 5 miles from the city. It has given vivid experiences to many thousands of people only in the country for a short time.

The Park has developed greatly in the past few years. Besides The Orphanage, where animals in distress are taken care of until they can be returned to the wild, there is an Educational Centre which provides vehicles to take school children around the park. It must have played a leading role in making the world in general aware of the importance of wildlife.

At the moment plans are in hand to purchase more land and so enlarge the Park. This is partly to give better protection from poaching and partly to make it a more contained ecological unit. It is absolutely imperative that wild animals have the full free range of all their food requirements, including that of minerals.

Political stability brought a tremendous boom in tourism and the government was able to increase the number of parks and reserves. However, forest excisions, the term used when land is taken away from the Forest Reserve, continued to be granted to an expanding clamorous population, and today there is much less forest than before Independence. The total forest area is less than 3 per cent of the country. Authority is well aware that this is less than in many European countries and there are hopeful signs that a much firmer stand will be made in the future over demands for forest land.

There are three big mountains in Kenya. Mount Kenya with an altitude of 17,058ft is the highest, and has its twin peaks of Nelion and Batian perpetually snow-capped. Mount Elgon is 14,178ft and has a crater with a diameter of more than seven miles. The Aberdare Mountain reaches a highest point of 13,120ft. All three are National Parks, Mount Elgon being gazetted as such only recently.

Mount Kenya National Park was, for many years, all that part of the mountain lying above the 11,000ft contour apart from two forested salients on the Naro Moru and Sirimon rivers. Recently the boundary was dropped 500ft but even so it is much too high to include many animals, and this park must be looked upon primarily as botanical (see map, pp 26–7).

Mount Elgon National Park is far from satisfactory. Half of that mountain lies in Uganda. To date there has been no indication that the Ugandan authorities will make a park or reserve of their half. Under such conditions it is extremely difficult to carry out efficient protection, for poachers cross the border and then escape because of the delay in obtaining police permission to follow.

The Aberdare National Park is given in present guide books as covering an area of 228 square miles. There have, however, been three recent additions which must bring this to nearly 300 square miles. The total mountain area is about 1,000. After traversing the length of the mountain the park swings downhill in a narrowing salient until, at the very tip, it ends at Treetops.

The Treetops Salient is the migration line along which the game in former years migrated from the two mountain masses of Kenya and Aberdare. Chief amongst these were the elephants, although buffalo also moved freely as did the bongo.

Today the farmland lying between the two mountains makes such movement almost impossible. Elephants still try, and very occasionally succeed, in their attempted migration. Another factor limiting migration is the Treetops ditch which was begun in 1956 and now extends for a length of about twenty miles.

Much of the vegetation in the Treetops Salient today consists of bush, secondary tree growth and Kikuyu grass. Some of this has been brought about by migrating elephants, especially along the actual route from The Ark to the boundary. Much more is the result of Kikuyu settlement of the last century which was stopped when the Forest Department took over at the beginning of the present century. One large area was cleared by the Forest Department for plantations in the forties and later abandoned. Finally, a fire in 1953 destroyed a considerable area of forest close to Treetops. The result of these complex combinations of forest destruction is that today we have a diversity of grassland, forest and bush in a high rainfall area. There is food for all, both grazers and browsers, and it has been stated that the Treetops Salient holds the biggest weight of game animals per acre of any area in the world.

Between 1952 and 1956 Kenya was enduring what was known as The Emergency. Most of the fighting between the Mau Mau and the British was in the forests. Although there was action in other forest areas, Mount Kenya and the Aberdares saw the greatest amount of fighting, with the most intense action taking place in the Treetops Salient. As usual the game suffered.

Thousands of snares were put down to obtain food. Bombs were dropped in large numbers by the RAF and mortar shells were fired by the army. Even the security forces themselves were not above potting at any animal they saw. The view has been expressed that, had The Emergency lasted for many more years, the East African bongo would have become extinct in its last great stronghold.

The mountain lying beneath the Aberdare National Park is divided into three hunting blocks, so that to some extent man can still play his vital role in the balance of Nature. To date no control work has been necessary within this park, other than disposing of the sick or wounded, which could become a menace to human life. After The Emergency animal populations increased, especially buffalo, but an optimum level appeared to be reached in the mid-sixties and there is no indication at present that the policy of non-interference will change.

The National Parks and Reserves of Kenya are not the ideal solution to the preservation of wildlife, for in them man is not allowed to play the part of a predator and so help to keep the balance as he has done in the past. But there is now no part of the world left where this could be so. Parks and reserves are the best that man can devise. Provided that they are never fenced, and that the huge overflow areas of the hunting blocks are maintained, then they can be a reasonable substitute for a true wilderness.

The National Parks then are the Noah's Arks of this modern world. It is appropriate that the Aberdare Mountain, and especially the Treetops Salient, with its history of animal migrations, of animal destruction and of human suffering, should be the site for another Ark—a physical Ark, built in the depths of the forest where tourists, the people whose money has poured into Kenya and so made the conservation of wildlife possible, can view them in comfort.

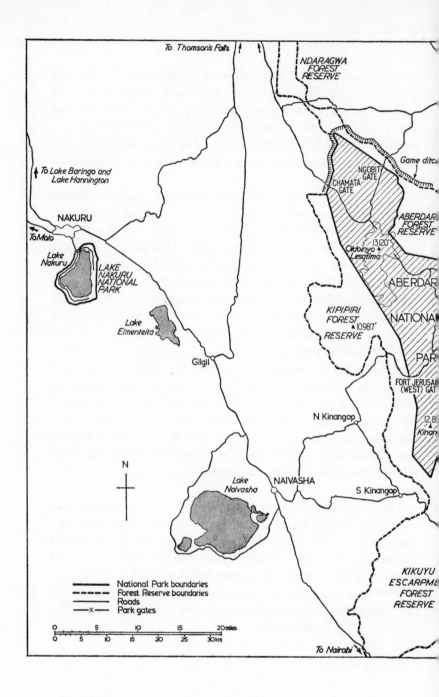

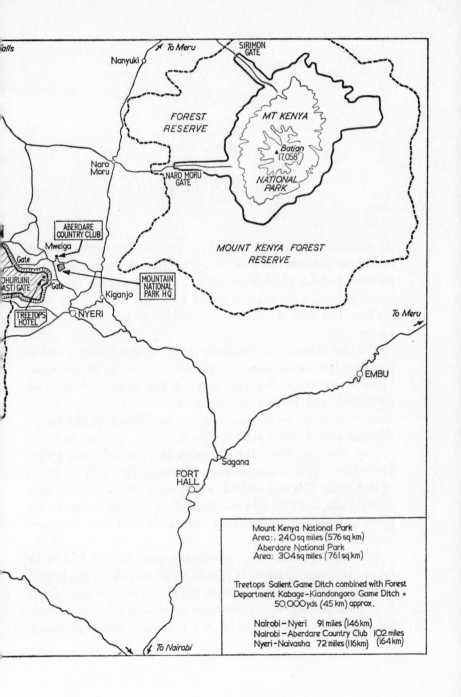

Mount Kenya National Park
Area: 240 sq miles (576 sq km)
Aberdare National Park
Area: 304 sq miles (761 sq km)

Treetops Salient Game Ditch combined with Forest
Department Kabage–Kiandongoro Game Ditch =
50,000 yds (45 km) approx.

Nairobi–Nyeri   91 miles (146 km)
Nairobi–Aberdare Country Club   102 miles
Nyeri–Naivasha   72 miles (116 km)   (164 km)

CHAPTER TWO

The Ark Is Built

At the time of writing (1973) The Ark has been open for just over three years. It has been navigated through turbulent seas of fortune. Indeed, there were times so turbulent that the faint-hearted thought the scheme would surely founder. Today all is set fair. The rains are over and a rainbow gives promise for the future.

The idea of building a game-viewing lodge much deeper within the Aberdare forest than the world-famous lodge at Treetops, came to a number of people when it was observed how close cultivation and human settlement were approaching. Positive action was taken in January 1967 by Bill Woodley, the Park's Warden and Kevin Lyons, owner of Steep, a large house at nearby Mweiga. They did not think in terms of a big lodge, just a fifteen-room construction sufficient to cope with the needs of that time. The mountain was searched from end to end for a suitable site, both on foot and from the air. Most attention was given to the Treetops Salient, so well known for its heavy game concentrations.

In choosing a site for a new lodge many factors had to be taken into consideration. It should be preferably in the habitat of those rare and unique animals, the bongo and the giant forest hog. Both are shy, forest creatures inhabiting the higher, more remote parts of the mountain. A grassy glade had to be found, with a permanent pool big enough to attract other forest animals. There had to be the possibilities of a good access road. Another must was a stream, near enough, and fast enough, to allow for operating hydraulic rams—much cheaper to install and maintain than engines—capable of lifting sufficient water to the building. This water would then be purified, stored and then gravity-fed to the lodge. And last but not least, a ridge had to be found whereon The Ark, as the lodge was later to be called, could finally rest as it did in the Bible.

The first choice was turned down on the grounds that it was too near Treetops. The second, discovered in April of that year, was, of course, known to the local Wakikuyu and went by the name of Yathabara—the Waterhole of the Leeches. What the Wanderobo, the original hunters in these forests, called it, does not appear to be known. Yathabara glade is about 9 miles from Treetops as the crow (or eagle) flies but is, of course, much farther by road.

In 1964, an area of 9 square miles adjacent to The Ark site had been surveyed by the Forest Department, and earmarked as non-essential for water catchment but suitable for 'Settlement'. This meant that it could be handed over to the Settlement Board, who would then divide it up and give it to landless Africans for cultivation. Thanks largely to the tireless efforts of Bill Woodley, this did not take place and the area, together with two other zones, was gazetted as a National Park in 1968. At that time the future of many areas of forest hung very much in the balance. Had the Aberdare National Park not acquired this land then The Ark could not have been built the following year. Indeed the whole Treetops Salient would have had a very insecure future.

Difficulties were encountered when it came to registration of the newly formed Company, chiefly on the grounds that the lodge would not be big enough. At this stage a professional

Danish hotelier of many years' experience, Mogens Soeborg, came upon the scene bringing with him promise of American finance on a massive scale, although this was later withdrawn.

In the battles which took place that summer between Mr Soeborg and the authorities to get the Company registered, it is to his credit that he insisted on a lodge deep within the forest. Most of Kenya's game-viewing lodges are near the boundary of the particular National Park, Reserve, or protected area in which they are sited. This has been done on the grounds of economy, both of transport and of time. The troubles arising from this mistaken policy are becoming more and more apparent. Salt, put down to attract the game, draws the animals away from the centre of the Park, which helps poachers living in the vicinity. It also means that over-grazing and over-browsing occurs, resulting in soil erosion.

The Ark is actually 4½ miles from the Park entrance, and those miles are a great attraction. Apart from the usual forest game seen feeding by the roadside, it is often blocked by huge herds of elephants, especially during the annual migrations. Cows with babies frequently demonstrate against the tourists' vehicles, usually with mock charges which end when the vehicles 'retreat'. Nevertheless these skirmishes give wonderful opportunities for photography.

The Company was eventually registered, first as Noah's Ark, and then simply as The Ark Ltd. The promise of big money having vanished, more had to come from other sources. It was found locally. Robin Higgin, Chairman of Mweiga Estates Ltd, joined the Company as Chairman, Mr Soeborg became Managing Director, and Mr Lyons joined the board. A number of professional hunters were allowed to join in and the Kenya Tourist Development Corporation subscribed for about 20 per cent of the shares. The original £90,000 (Kenya) rose to £160,000 when a bank loan was raised. It was decided that the lodge should have fifty-seven beds and from then on the project became a reality.

The Waterhole of the Leeches is 7,600ft above sea level, near an old elephant trail which starts on the moorlands near Satima. The bulk of the elephants went through Nyeri Forest, then on to Mt Kenya. Some, however, went down on to Cole's Plain and crossed this huge expanse by following the riverine forests of the Moyo, Amboni, Ngare Nyiro and Burguret. It is still quite easy to find where these trails enter the Mt Kenya forests. Whenever possible elephants choose ridge country for migrations which enables them to detect enemies from afar. There is little doubt that the road now leading up from Mweiga village to the National Park entrance was also part of a trail. Although the countryside is now under agriculture, it was formerly a forest; much of it runs along a ridge with a deep gorge on either side.

This migration trail between the two mountain masses of Kenya and Aberdares was used chiefly by elephants, but other game animals also migrated, especially when populations became dense. These would include buffalo and, to a lesser extent, rhino and even bongo. The eland today do not leave the sanctuary of the moorlands of the Aberdares but, in former times, they may well have been much more migratory as, for example, they are on Mt Kenya today. In view of the fact that Cole's Plain was teeming with zebra only thirty years ago it is strange that they are so localised on the Aberdares.

During the Kenya Emergency this elephant trail was used a lot by both the Mau Mau and the British. Later it was opened up by the National Parks to allow their anti-poaching patrols to be more mobile. It was, however, still only a grass track during the time The Ark was being built, and remained so for some months after it was opened. The National Parks undertook the work of laying down murram—soil with a very high iron ore content—

31

along its full length from entrance gate to building. Many culverts were also put in. From a point just above The Ark, where it touches 8,oooft, to the moorlands there is just a game trail. From the gate to The Ark the road is for use by Company vehicles only, and not to be used by others without permission.

The Ark can truly be said to be an international building. Graham McCullough, a Scot living in Nairobi, was chosen to be the architect. After several attempts, he finally produced a plan of a building we now know as The Ark which the directors accepted with alacrity. A Swede, Lars Hanson, was the interior designer. Karta Singh, an Asian contractor living in Nyeri, did the actual construction. How well he built is there for all to see. An Austrian chef, Eddie Knodl, recruited and trained local staff, starting two months before the opening date.

Work began on 3 February 1969 and the first guests arrived just over ten months later! It is true that the rains failed that year. It is also true that to achieve such speed entailed a lot of overtime and hard work.

All the main timbers and the roofing shingles were cut from cedar trees growing on Mt Kenya 60 miles away. The stone for the walls and the foundations came from Nyeri, 20 miles distant. The artistic sandstone used for lining the walls of the viewing lounge and around the fireplace is from a quarry near Mombasa, some 300 miles away. Much of the furniture is made from muminga, *Pterocarpus angolensis*, a Tanzanian timber. The interior wood is cypress which is grown in local plantations.

Special features of The Ark are the huge stone fireplace, in the lounge, which can take logs like tree trunks, and a photographic hide at ground-level. The fireplace has an electric extractor fan to ensure smoke will not enter the room. In a building carefully sound-proofed this is most important. The hide, or dungeon, as it is more affectionately known, is circular with slotted open windows wide enough to give an adequate photographic field, but not big enough to allow animals to enter.

The big artificial 'moons', kept on all night, are some of the most powerful in the country. After The Ark had been operating a year, Kodak gave special advice which enabled three more of these special lights to be added, but these are only switched on when animals of importance are within range.

The building is carpeted throughout with thick modern squares which effectively reduce sound to a minimum. A buzzer system is installed in every room which, when switched on, sounds to waken sleeping guests as soon as a rare animal enters the viewing area.

Electricity is generated by diesel-driven engines in a power-house about 300yd up the hill where a baffle system reduces noise to a minimum. Cooking is by gas. All the facilities are available for guests to stay more than one night without having to return to the Country Club base.

The Club, originally called Steep, was the home of Ark director Kevin Lyons and his wife Trim. Built by Lyons's mother in the late 1930s on the lines of an English country house, Steep stands on a 1,300-acre estate, amid some of the loveliest scenery in Kenya. The Company took it over on a share exchange basis. Whilst the Country Club's amenities are limited at present they will doubtless increase with time. Over 4 miles of river on the estate have been stocked with rainbow trout and 2lb specimens are now sometimes taken. What was once a wired-in orchard has been turned into an aviary.

The Club is residential, but at the moment has only accommodation for ten people. There are plans for big expansions. Undoubtedly its quiet beauty will be much more appreciated as it becomes better known.

Remembering the original state of the road, nothing more than a grass track, it is a wonder that all the building materials ever reached the site at all. There were troubles, of course. Vehicles often stuck in the mud and staff were chased by wild animals more than once.

Even so, the handing over ceremony by Mr Singh took place on 7 October 1969, three weeks ahead of schedule. Between then and the arrival of the first guests at midday on 22 November, the staff were frantically trying to put everything ship-shape—or rather Ark-shape. So late was the arrival of some of the crockery and furniture from Mombasa that it was still being uncrated only an hour or so before the visitors arrived.

November is the month of the short rains and the first drops fell as the new arrivals were hurrying along the gangplank. This 400ft structure among the beautiful golden flowers of the cassia bushes, sometimes called the catwalk, has become a favourite place for birdwatchers. Starting at ground level, the plank ends at the drawbridge leading on to the after deck. This bridge is not raised until dark, so guests can freely use the gangplank in its entire length until night falls. Besides its game and bird viewing attractions, the walk also helps to prevent congestion within the building when there is a full house.

During those early days there were plenty of teething troubles. The 4½-mile forest track, for instance, could become very sticky at that time of year. The Ark maintains contact with base by radio, generates its own electricity, and pumps and purifies its own water. It cooks its own food and the guests' breakfast before they leave. It was thus understandable that the management did not at first engage outside hunters and hostesses. I joined the Company as Hunter Guide a few days after The Ark opened.

At that time the glade was exactly as Nature made it. The rush-fringed pool in the centre had a yard-wide path all round it where each day we scattered two buckets of salt to attract game. We never expected then to see animals close to the building. Indeed we were thankful to see any animals at all! All the

34

Page 35 Two of the crowned cranes that decorate the lawns of the Aberdare Country Club. These beautiful birds, 3½ft-tall, being quite tame are favourite subjects for photographers

Page 36 The slayers and the slain

activity had naturally disturbed the glade and its residents so that it took about three months for the animals to get used to the new situation. They were all extremely wild. Nervous rhino would come, holding their snouts high. At 50yd from the building they would about-turn and lumber off, invariably taking every other animal away with them. When the first bongo came a few months later, the duty hunter led his few guests into the viewing lounge on their hands and knees. Despite this, the first click of a camera caused the lovely animal to bound away into the night.

The words of my poem, 'No man-made machine has defiled this land', were true for just two years. By then both elephants and buffalo had entered the glade by the hundred. Elephants like a great deal of soil with their salt. One night, during their migrations, 235 of the great pachyderms were counted. Buffalo wallow a great deal, carrying mud away from the pool on their bodies which they later knock off on the bushes. The National Parks estimated that hundreds of tons of soil had been removed from in front of the building. If this were to continue, it would not only undermine The Ark, but cause a swamp that would prevent leopards coming near. It was essential to return the soil which meant using a bulldozer.

The Ark has been built with a view to reducing the danger from wild animals as far as possible. There is no long walk-in, just a short step from the vehicle park to the gangplank. Elderly, sick or infirm people can be transported to the double doors, or 'tradesman's entrance' at the back. So far The Ark has not had to kill an elephant to save any guest's life as unfortunately was necessary at Treetops in 1968.

It is not possible to build a lodge in the middle of big-game country without some element of risk. For this reason, all guests must sign that they do not hold the Company responsible, and that they enter the National Park at their own risk. The road to

C

The Ark passes through some of the densest type of forest in Africa. Unlike travel in thorn-bush country, a vehicle is unable to take any evasive action.

When the road was being surveyed from the point where it leaves the elephant trail to The Ark site, one of the directors,

To Dick
Happy New Year
Napier Dunn
The Ark

Dick Prickett, drawn at The Ark in 1972 by Napier Dunn, illustrator for *Mananchi Daily News*, Tokyo, Japan

Kevin Lyons, marching ahead through the bush, was attacked by an old buffalo bull. He was hooked, lifted on to its head and carried some distance. The armed Park Ranger with the party dared not fire to kill for fear of hitting the man, so fired into the air instead. At the report, the beast tossed his victim aside and ran off. The injuries, fortunately, were not serious.

Another morning, guests were filing out to the vehicles when a buffalo bull dashed through the line, scattering people, bags and cases. The fattest man there was reported to be the first back into The Ark.

However, there have been serious charges by both elephant and rhino where speed on the part of the vehicle was essential. Rhino in particular are liable to carry a charge through. There were those who were adamant that The Ark could not be a success. Smoke, human odour at ground-level and the inevitable noises from the kitchen, were something new in the field of game viewing. The whole venture was therefore something of a gamble, a gamble which, I am pleased to say, has more than paid off.

CHAPTER THREE

Trees That Grow near The Ark

The indigenous forests of Kenya lie mostly in the area known as The Highlands. Although they comprise 12 per cent of the fertile land, they form less than 3 per cent of the country as a whole, for one must not forget the vast semi-desert areas of the Northern Frontier. This is much lower than most European or American countries and great attempts are being made today to increase the area by plantations. The Aberdare Mountain is in the heart of The Highlands with the equator running across the northern section.

In a tropical country there is always a dense carpet of bush beneath the canopy of all but the most perfect stands of timber. This is because the light intensity is so great and is present for so much of the year. Also the temperature and rainfall encourage fast growth. As a result the soil becomes rich with the leaf-fall of millions of years.

The local people have always looked to the forests for their cultivation. They have cleared small areas by fire, cultivated a few crops, and moved on. Nature has then healed the scars and made the land fertile again. Today there is no possibility that people will cultivate and move on. Indeed, there is a never-ending cry to cut down the trees as some people believe indigenous forests should be replaced by farmland or regimented plantations, yielding nothing but farm produce or factory timber.

The forested areas of the Aberdares lie between 6,000–9,000ft in what is termed a mist-belt, which comes after the long rains. In a bad year the mist lasts from about the middle of May to the middle of August, and can be most depressing. Nevertheless, even during this period of cold and damp, there are often days of beautiful sunshine. The rains fall largely at night and are sufficient to last through the long dry months of January, February and March. September and October can also be very fine months. The short rains, which usually start in the latter half of November and are over by Christmas, are not reliable.

Of all the indigenous trees of the Kenyan Highlands, unquestionably the most impressive and valuable is the Pencil Cedar, *Juniperus procera*. Actually, it is not a cedar at all but the largest species of juniper in the world, growing to a height of 120ft. Cedar has a fine aromatic timber and is impervious to the ravages of white ants. Consequently it has been used on a vast scale, both for building construction and fencing posts. It was used extensively in pencil making but the introduction of the cheap ball-point pen has nearly ended that industry. At one time also there was a considerable demand for cedar oil, extracted as a by-product at the mills.

Cedar is a tree of the drier mountains. It cannot be seen along the road to The Ark although the cedar zone commences at this latitude and the number of trees progressively increases towards the drier north. They are common at Thomson's Falls and along that part of the mountain constituting the eastern wall of the Great Rift Valley. Cedar is prevalent all over Mount Kenya and some of the stands are very fine indeed. Once these huge stands, produced by Nature over hundreds of years, are cut out, it is difficult to see how the timber can be replaced economically, valuable as it may be. Cedar is very difficult to grow in plantations as it is extremely slow-growing, suffering greatly from heartrot and ingrowing bark.

Cedar has been described as a decadent species. It is difficult

41

for us to realise that tree species do not last forever, but they do not, any more than do animal species.

Two other softwood trees almost as common in The Highlands as cedar are *Podocarpus gracilior* and *P. milanjianus* which look alike. The species growing at the top of the hill just before descending to The Ark is *P. milanjianus*. Both are evergreens with distinct needles and grow to a height of 100ft or more. They have a fine timber, superior for building purposes to the pines more commonly used. In the timber trade both are known as East African Yellow-Wood and, like the cedar, neither can be produced well in plantations. Fast-growing exotic cypresses and pines are usually found in plantations.

The most common trees to be found all the way along the road leading from the National Park entrance to The Ark itself are the many different species of *Cassipourea*, usually Pillar-wood, *Cassipourea malosana*, and the Brown Olive, *Olea africana*. *Cassipourea* species are not used commercially to any extent. Brown Olive, however, is a fine cabinet timber and makes superlative slow-burning firewood. It is a small tree with dark green leaves. At certain times of the year the brown olives growing near the Country Club attract great numbers of hornbills of various species to feed on the fruit. Although not edible to humans the fruit is much appreciated by monkeys as well as birds.

Kenya has many beautiful indigenous trees, though not many are to be found close to The Ark because of the altitude. Nandi Flame, *Spathodea nilotica*, grows in the vicinity of the Country Club. This tree has multi-globulets of brick-red flowers 5in long. Many of the other beautiful flowering trees have no European names; only the tongue-twisting Latin, or the equally alien vernacular of the local tribes. Such is *Cordia abyssinica* with its masses of snow-white blossoms, and *Albizia gummifera* with wondrous deep green leaves and a crown when flowering like apple blossom. Those trees may be seen on the roadside when travelling to the Country Club from Nyeri. Both trees are usually known by the first half of the Latin name.

A strange, but beautiful tree, common all over the Aberdares and which again has no common name is *Olinia usambarensis.* This is the tree growing on the low side of the catwalk when entering The Ark. Its timber has no value but, in the dry season, the old leaves fall and the new flush has a most entrancing red colour, making the tree perceptible many miles away.

The most beautiful tree which is truly indigenous to the area is the Cape Chestnut, *Calodendrum capense,* which has masses of delicate pink flowers. It is found all over the Nyeri area and is the most conspicuous of the trees on the lawns of the Country Club. The chestnut can be seen in ones and twos all over the country-side leading up to the National Park entrance. Once inside the forest it is found in declining size and magnificence as the road climbs towards the 7,000ft contour. None occur above that altitude.

The Highlands of Kenya above 8,000ft are covered with hundreds of square miles of bamboo. When leaving The Ark, one can see this zone as a paler green colour in the far distance. However, one must know where to look and not confuse the bamboo with the brighter green of the bush areas. The zone extends to an altitude of nearly 10,000ft, when the bamboo becomes stunted and finally gives way to the grass of the moorlands. This is Mountain Bamboo, quite different from that found in Asia. It is *Arundinaria alpina,* completely green and growing to a height of nearly 6oft. From above the bamboo is a waving sea of pale-green feathery tops. Below is a fantastic tangle of giant reed-like stems, some in the peak of their vigour, others standing brown and dead, ready to snap with a loud report and come crashing down upon the head of the first intruder. Wherever a gap has formed and lets in the light, spear-like points of new shoots grow, ready to take up the everlasting battle for survival.

To date no real utilisation of this tremendous volume of produce has taken place. Paper has been made from it, of fair quality, but there is a complete lack of transport systems: no smooth-flowing rivers exist, as in Asia, and there are no roads.

The bamboo forests are dark, cold, and at some times of the year constantly dripping from the mist. This is a land of weird creaks and groans whenever the wind rises and rubs the stems together. Often the wet percolates through the tiny holes made by beetles in the stems and, by cutting off just above a nodule, it is possible to obtain a cool drink. Strangely the Mountain Bamboo only flowers about the fifteenth year, after which areas sometimes extending to hundreds of acres will die en mass.

There is not a great deal of wildlife in the bamboo forests for they are too cold, dark and wet. Apart from the spears of the new shoots, and in clearings, there is little food. However, they have acted as a refuge for the bongo whenever it has been heavily hunted. Only in recent years has this shy creature been found in numbers in areas of open bush such as the vicinity of The Ark. Elephants during migrations will enter the bamboo but they do not stay there. Buffalo, like bongo, use it as a place of refuge and the cows often go there alone to calve.

In sheltered places on the Aberdares can be found wild bananas, *Ensete ventricosum*. The huge leaves, sometimes 8ft long and 2ft wide, are often used as makeshift umbrellas during the rains. They also make a durable thatch. Cultivated bananas are of Malaysian origin. When I was a forester at Kiandongoro ('place of the bongo') 10 miles from The Ark, I saw many wild bananas in the Chania Valley. Once a year, just when the plants were fruiting, the elephants would sweep down the length of the valley, eating and smashing them all as they went.

Figs, found all over the country, also grow near The Ark. There are many species. The majority start life as epiphytes—

they embrace another tree, then take over and become self-supporting after the death of their host. Fig trees are all useless as either timber or firewood, but they provide useful shade and have the rare property of allowing crops to be grown in their vicinity. Some are revered by local tribes as abodes of departed spirits and are frequently used as local gathering grounds. One, The Bark Cloth Fig, *Ficus natalensis*, has been much used in Uganda to make bark cloth dresses. This is the species used for the souvenir menus at The Ark. The bast, or underbark, is boiled and then beaten to the required size and thickness.

Visitors to The Ark are always impressed by the many flowering shrubs. Probably the commonest is the *Cassias*. The species which, twice a year, throws an aura of gold around the building is *Cassia didymobotrya*, a dense, light green bush with bright yellow flowers looking rather like candles capped by blackish brown snuffers. Another very beautiful flowering shrub is the Cape Lilac, *Vernonia brachycalyx*. The florets are a brilliant violet when they first open but exposure to the bright sunshine soon makes them fade and the bush then looks extremely scruffy. Another species, with white flowers, is not as common.

The bushes which grow near the vehicle yard above The Ark are Lion's Claw, *Crotalaria agatiflora*. The claw-shaped flowers are yellow-green. The pods are also yellow, up to 3in long, with a distinct beak or curved tip. From the catwalk of The Ark can be seen other conspicuous bushes with yellow berries. These are Sodom Apple, *Solanum aculeastrum*. The young branches are armed with strong curved prickles which tear the clothes to shreds, and the lemon-yellow berries or fruit are extremely bitter. The flowers are very similar to that of the potato.

In the Highland forests a few days after the rains break, appears one of Kenya's most beautiful flowers—the Fireball, *Haemanthus multiflorus*. Bulbous plants, with globular flowers of brilliant red and gold the size of a tennis ball on foot-high stalks, they are usually to be found in groups of up to half a dozen. Their delicate beauty is breath-taking. A few can usually be seen by the roadside between the National Park's entrance gate and The Ark itself, and there is a small group in the thick bush opposite the viewing lounge. The Fireball only blossom for a week or so, and are then seen no more until the advent of the next rains. More rarely they can also be found in the drier bush country.

All over the clearings in the forest can be found a less agreeable plant, the Kenya nettle. This grows to a height of 10ft and its poisonous hairs are extremely painful. The excavations for the foundations of The Ark brought in masses of the plant and it was cut down once a month. No animal appears to touch the nettle once it attains full stature but elephants love it when young and tender. They soon found the plant at The Ark and from that time there was no need to do further cutting. In fact, there is very little of the nettle left today. With that strange perversity of Nature, the leaves of the nettle when boiled are a recognised diet of many African tribes, while the bulbs of the Fireball are poisonous. . . .

CHAPTER FOUR

Beasts That Walk near The Ark

The animals of the forests around The Ark game-viewing lodge are not all true forest species. The indigenous forest is not, as is so often imagined, a mass of tall trees standing shoulder to shoulder. There are sometimes glades of thin or poor soil within the forest which extend for hundreds of acres. In these glades may be found animals normally associated with the plains and indeed usually referred to as 'plains game'.

On the moorlands above The Ark can be found lion, serval cat, zebra, eland and reedbuck. With the exception of the two lions recorded soon after The Ark opened, none of these animals has been seen in the vicinity. The attraction of salt could very well alter this.

ELEPHANT (*Loxodonta africana*) Unquestionably the elephant is the lord of creation and to watch his stately, deliberate, smooth-flowing walk is to feel that he is aware of his status. At one time he roamed over the whole of Kenya, the forests, the plains, and even across the desert areas of the frontier. Today his movements have been drastically curtailed, but even now he often makes determined efforts to revisit old areas, sometimes with tragic results.

Elephants that are truly wild are difficult to weigh and even more difficult to measure accurately. An average adult bull stands 10ft 6in at the shoulder and weighs 5¾ tons. However, a specimen was shot in the Cuando River region of south-western Angola on 13 November 1955 which was very much bigger. It was estimated to stand 12ft 9in and to weigh 10·7 tons. Details of this huge beast can be found in *The Guinness Book of Records*. Another elephant reputed to stand over 12ft at the shoulder was last seen in Rhodesia in January 1965, and may well be the largest living land animal.

The heaviest pair of tusks are in the British Natural History Museum in London and weigh 226 and 214lb.

The African elephant is much larger than his Asiatic cousin. Most noticeable differences are the African elephant's huge ears, horizontal back, much bigger tusks, and total aversion to work. The Belgians had a training school in the Congo which proved that the taming of the African elephant was possible, but they had to admit that the cost of training far outweighed the benefits. Hannibal, when he crossed the Alps, would possibly have admitted the same.

Although science does not recognise two species of African elephant, there is a great difference between those found in the forest and those on the plains. The former are usually referred to as bush elephants and are distinctly smaller, have pointed ears and carry much smaller tusks, supposedly because of the lack of minerals in forest areas.

During the past few years the myth that elephants live for hundreds of years has been exploded. The elephant's life-span is much the same as man's. Indeed, their whole social behaviour is so reminiscent of man himself that the Wameru tribe refuse to eat elephant meat, declaring 'Ndovu sawa sawa mtu' (the elephant is like a man). An interesting feature of elephant herds is that they keep cohesion in dense bush and forests, no matter how far apart the individual members are scattered. This is achieved by a brown fluid exuding from a gland near the ear. The fluid becomes

48

smeared on passing leaves and, although the smell cannot be detected by man, apparently other elephants have little difficulty in following it.

A factor limiting the life-span of elephants is the teeth formation. There are six teeth on each side of both jaws. Each tooth, about a foot long, is comprised of a number of vertical plates cemented together and capable of withstanding terrific grinding pressures. As each front tooth becomes worn out through taking the brunt of the work, it is replaced by the one behind moving forward. When all six have thus been worn away the elephant must, of necessity, die of starvation. The crowns of these teeth are marked by a row of lozenge-shaped dark areas.

The myth of elephant 'graveyards' has also been disproved. The reason why so many dead elephants have been found in one area is because, in times of drought, they congregate round the fast-drying waterholes. Vast numbers create a muddy quagmire so that many of the youngsters and the aged become stuck and finally die. Should the area then dry out completely it may look very much like a graveyard, and doubtless many of the early explorers mistook such places as just that.

The reasons why very few elephant remains are found are two-fold. Ivory rots in the open very quickly and is also nibbled extensively by porcupines. Predators carry away all but the skull and the largest of the leg-bones and these soon become overgrown with grass fertilised by the final remains. Often, as death approaches, the elephant totters down some ravine to the little stream at the bottom. There he finally dies at the water's edge. The floods come and the body becomes silted over at some bend in the stream.

The most wonderful part of an elephant's anatomy is its trunk which has a tremendous number of nerves. Its uses are almost equal to that of the human hand. Not only does the elephant gather together the grass and foliage upon which it feeds with its

49

trunk but it will chastise the young with it and also fondle the partner in courtship.

The gestation period of elephants is normally 22 months and may extend to two years. Twins are rare. The baby suckles by turning back the trunk and using its mouth in the normal fashion. The mother's two teats are situated between the fore-legs and are pendulous. For the first few months the infant spends virtually the whole of the time beneath the mother's stomach and the rest of the herd keep very close. It is not unusual to see a female elephant accompanied by up to three youngsters of different ages.

Most elephants are right-tusked and, through constant dig-ging, this tusk becomes a few pounds lighter than its companion. The nerve in the tusk is a conical-shaped mass of red, jelly-like substance, reaching sometimes more than half the length. Be-cause of this variance it is very difficult to guess the weight of tusks accurately. Many Africans are extremely superstitious about seeing it and turn the head away when it is being pulled out.

A great deal of soil is continually eaten by elephants. This may act as a purgative and it may also help in the digestion of the huge quantity of foliage and grass eaten almost continuously. A certain amount of salt and other mineral matter is also obtained this way. A big bull elephant can eat as much as 600lb of green matter every 24 hours. This is why they are always on the move—to avoid undue devastation of any one area. Elephants are both browsers and grazers. They will push over quite big trees to reach the fruit or fresh foliage at the top and also strip the bark for tannin. Long grass they pull out in trunkfulls but when it is short they first ridge it together with their feet. Recent research has shown that where elephants have been over-protected they have destroyed the forests and more grass has grown, with resultant heart troubles and breeding failures. This is because grass does not contain sufficient protein.

Before the invention of gunpowder and the subsequent mass slaughter of elephants, the huge animals played a vital part in the complicated balance of Nature. They did not 'destroy' trees but simply turned forest into bush and grass so that the smaller denizens of the wild could live. Moreover, by making their paths along the contours of the hills and, by dribbling down an unending stream of leaves and twigs as they fed, elephants ensured that soil erosion did not take place.

It is interesting to reflect that, had it not been for the well-defined trails through the forest and dense bush, penetration of Africa could not have taken place with the speed that it did in the middle of the last century. In forests where elephants and other big game no longer exist, huge sums of money have to be spent just to create pathways which, in six months, will be covered over once more.

There are a number of reasons why men are not killed as frequently by elephants as by buffalo. Because of its huge bulk, the elephant can very often be detected at a considerable distance, even in thick cover. Detection is also helped by the constant noise of tummy rumblings, evacuations, and the breaking down of foliage. Once an elephant is located, and provided it is alone, it is comparatively easy to approach to within a few yards. Its eyesight is so weak that everything beyond about 50yd is only a blur.

Control of elephants has to be carried out from time to time as they can do disastrous damage to crops. In spite of its huge bulk, an elephant usually goes straight down if the bullet is placed correctly. It does not appear to be able to withstand the shock of modern rifles to the same degree as buffalo. The brain shot is difficult and is only carried out successfully by experienced hunters, the heart shot is simple and the target area is big.

A favourite shot of scouts on government control work is into the ear orifice. All the bones of elephant are of a honey-comb formation which gives a lightweight strength ratio to carry the immense weight of the animal. Above the brain is an area of perforated bone which looks just like a lorry radiator, and which may be up to 18in deep. Doubtless this is a help in pushing over small trees when feeding. A bullet placed there does not appear to give the animal even a headache, and it takes a very experienced hunter to know just where this area ends and the brain begins.

It is impossible to make an accurate census in the dense type of forest covering so much of the Aberdare Mountains, but it is thought by the Park Warden that about 3,000 elephants are now living there.

BLACK RHINOCEROS (*Diceros bicornis*) Of the two species of rhino, the Black and the White, only the black is native to Kenya. Half a dozen white have been brought up recently from South Africa and released in the Meru National Park, where they doubtless once abounded, but the success of the experiment has yet to be proved. Both names are ridiculous and have no bearing on colour, as the two animals are a uniform shade of grey, merging to brown. The black is also known as the 'Hook-lipped rhinoceros' which is much more descriptive and it is a great pity the name is not in more general use. The white rhino is supposed to have gained its name from the Afrikaans word 'Wyt' which means 'Wide' and doubtless referred to the great square mouth. Indeed, the white rhino has often been called the wide-mouthed rhino.

Of the two rhinos the black is by far the most common. It has been, and still is, ruthlessly killed for the sake of its horn which is then smuggled out of the country and sold to certain elderly gentlemen in the East who endow it with powers as an aphrodisiac. The fact that the horns can be cut into small pieces and hidden in, say, a bag of beans makes their smuggling out much

Page 53 Two of The Ark's regulars: *(above)* Large-spotted genet coming for its nightly feed; *(below)* Old Dewlap, the fearless buffalo bull. The large fold of skin hanging from the throat shows just why he was given the nickname

Page 54 (above) A 16ft reticulated giraffe in the Samburu Game Reserve
Page 55 (opposite) Masai giraffes in a 'necking' duel. These fights, exclusive
to the males, decide which should have dominance over the harem

Page 56 (*above*) Common waterbuck; (*below*) Coke's hartebeest

easier than ivory. For a long time it used to be believed that the horn is not true horn but compressed hairs. Latest scientific research, however, confirms that the horn is like a toe-nail. Where protection is effective the rhino, black or white, holds its own well and is in no immediate danger.

Ultimate danger to the rhino usually comes from the expanding human population and the habitat destruction which follows. Nearly a thousand of these great pachyderms had to be shot after the last war to accommodate the expanding Wakamba tribe.

The black rhino, the one found at The Ark, is much smaller than the white, and it is doubtful if the largest males ever weigh a full 2 tons. It is far less placid in temperament than the white and, over the years, has killed many people. Much of this alleged aggression, however, can be attributed to poor eyesight, an intense curiosity, and to the fact that in dense bush there is no room on the path for both his vast bulk and a fleeing man.

Black rhino are browsers but the white is a true grazer. This probably is the cause of the difference in the period of gestation, the black being sixteen months to the nine of the white. A strange difference between the black and the white rhino is that the calf of the white always precedes the dam, being guided by pressures of the long posterior horn, whereas the calf of the black trots obediently behind.

Both black and white are much infested with ticks and the tick bird, a species of starling, performs the dual role of relieving its host of these parasites and giving warning of impending danger. Both species also use a special midden to deposit their droppings and then scatter them with their hind feet. All rhinos carry a sore behind the shoulder, more pronounced in some than in others. This is purely superficial and confined to the epidermis. It is associated and involved with the life cycle of a species of fly. During part of this cycle the fly is in the scattered droppings of the rhino's own dung. The degree of inflammation depends on

D   57

the cycle stage of the fly and also the attentions of the ever-present tick birds.

In addition to the usual snortings and blowings the black rhino has a high-pitched squeak which sounds most incongruous for a beast of such size.

The population of black rhino on the whole of the Aberdare Mountain is thought to be now over 2,000.

AFRICAN BUFFALO (*Syncerus caffer*) Visitors to Kenya usually refer to the great black buffaloes they see as 'water' buffaloes. The domestic water buffalo in Africa is found only in Egypt and the Sudan but the wild buffalo, first discovered at the Cape by the Dutch, is found over most areas south of the Sahara. Its total population in Africa is believed to be between two and three million.

The buffalo is not indigenous to Africa as no bones have ever been found in prehistoric diggings. These animals are believed to have moved south into the continent from Asia millions of years ago. The little red 'bush cow' of West Africa is undoubtedly the most primitive form, and there is also a dwarf buffalo in the Sudan. As with so many animals, the buffalo reaches its greatest size in South Africa, but the record heads are to be found on Mount Kenya and the adjacent Aberdare Mountains.

Towards the close of the nineteenth century an outbreak of rinderpest broke out amongst all cloven-hoofed wild mammals near the point of contact with domestic stock in North Eastern Africa. It was most severe in the buffalo herds, sweeping through them all the way to the Cape. According to Rowland Ward, the epidemic was most severe in East Africa, where the survival rate was put at less than one in *ten thousand*. It speaks volumes for the vitality and reproductive powers of this animal that, after only a few decades, the herds were back to normal.

Buffalo are extremely fond of wallowing in mud and will trek considerable distances both morning and night to suitable places. They are found in every type of habitat from the moorlands at 10,000ft altitude, to the steamy papyrus swamps at the coast; from dense tropical forest to the sandy wastes of the Kenya frontier, provided water is within reach.

Perhaps more people have been killed in Africa by the buffalo than any other animal and he has acquired a fearsome reputation. Yet the vast majority of buffalo are not ill-disposed to man and run away when disturbed. Even when wounded they do not always attack. Some old bulls living a solitary life do, however, become bad-tempered. Most buffalo when not severely hunted are extremely curious of behaviour they do not understand, and can be drawn quite close by waving a handkerchief on a stick. However, it is unwise to let them get too near.

The buffalo is such a dangerous adversary when wounded because his faculties of hearing, seeing and smelling are developed to a remarkable degree so that he is quite capable of circling and taking his enemy from behind. He is also one of the few animals habitually to look above his own height and to keep his head high when charging. His brain is protected by a boss that only the heaviest bullet can penetrate and his heart, frontally, is similarly protected by a massive dewlap. Once worked up into an absolute frenzy a buffalo is capable of absorbing bullet after bullet into the heart with no immediate effect. His hide is extremely thick and tough and he does not readily succumb to shock. A bull can reach a ton in weight, and with so many fighting qualities it is small wonder that hunters hold him in such high esteem.

One of my most vivid memories is of a buffalo hunt, with dogs, when doing control work in the mid-sixties. We found the spoor of a bull and his cow companion in the maize and followed into the depths of the forest. The procedure was for Mohamed, my trained companion at that time, to move slowly, eyes fixed on the ground. I would be just behind, covering him with the rifle against the unexpected, and the pack would be trailing behind. The farther we proceeded that day the denser became the cover and by midday, when the spoor led into the really thick stuff, I was tense and ready.

Warning would always come when the first buffalo rose to its feet some 50yd ahead. Buffalo always lie-up for the day in a circle and it is rare to get much nearer. One had then to jump smartly off the trail as the dogs swept excitedly past. Then I would run, with the rifle at the ready, so that when the dogs bayed I was close enough to shoot before the buffalo could break.

This particular morning all the pack apart from Mackendi Muncher, the perky little sheepdog, rushed a bushbuck. Mackendi went in a different direction and found the buffalo alone. When the dog bayed, Mohamed Bule, who was half my age, forgot his instructions and raced through the forest, leaving me panting behind. In a grassy clearing stood the huge bull, with Mackendi frantically barking in front of his lowered head. His consort, an in-season cow, stood behind. Mohamed realised at once that he had done wrong in leaving me and, upon reaching the scene, crouched behind the trunk of a fallen cedar tree.

At that moment the buffalo caught sight of him and came at a heavy gallop. Mackendi Muncher earned his name by gripping the bull's testicles and hanging on. The cow followed. Reaching the great log the bull got his forelegs over, then Mohamed fired three times whilst the cow was pushing and prodding the old bull from behind. Soon it was all over. The two beasts cleared the log and, in the melee, Mohamed was trodden on the leg and little Mackendi Muncher was scraped off. Why the bull did not stop to vent his rage we shall never know. Possibly the cow was chivvying too much from behind. Or, he may have respected those sharp teeth of the dog.

We couldn't find a drop of blood. Nevertheless we followed

the bull's heavy footprints until dark. Mohamed was limping but I was so infuriated with his lack of self-discipline that I had no patience to do more than glance at his bruises. At the end of the day I blazed the last tree and was back at first light. Mohamed did not complain though he must have been in considerable pain. Again we found no blood and again I blazed a tree at nightfall.

The next day was spent in a general search of the whole area. We were actually heading back for the vehicle when the dogs, which we thought were all behind us, broke into the welcome music of a bay. The intense, high-pitched barking came from a low patch of creeper-covered bush at the foot of the slope. As we stood hesitating, the noise stopped abruptly.

Then it happened. With a crash the bull broke cover, possibly a ton of mud-splattered muscle and flesh moving forward like a tank, taking the bushes in his stride. With head held high and huge horns widespread he was a sight to be fixed in the memory as long as life should last. He was upon us before I could even swing the rifle up clean, and both barrels blasted him point-blank. The huge bull did not appear to flinch and, for a second, I looked into eyes big and round in a body invincible.

I jumped off the track and, as I did so, my one thought was 'God, has Mohamed been flattened?'. Next moment the answer came with the boom of a rifle. From the ground I looked across the track and there was Mohamed on his knees. The big bull had passed between us and, as the bushes swallowed him up, Mohamed had put one barrel into his buttocks, a shot which doubtless slowed him down. The whole pack was pouring noisily between us and, farther on, they held the buffalo once more in noisy bay. There were other noises too. The snorting and grunting, tail swishing and stamping of a badly hit buffalo bull at long last making his final stand.

We tiptoed, rifles ready, over ground soaked with blood. Only by kneeling side by side could we see him a few yards away. Fear gripped us, for we both knew that, badly wounded as he was, he was now a fighting fury and, should he see or smell us, would come straight through the pack. We fired together for the heart. Not once but over and over again. A feeling of hopelessness came over me, a feeling that we were up against something that just would not go down. Then the vast bulk toppled over. The bushes on the slope gave way under his weight and he rolled over and over. Again we both had to jump as the body came to rest between us. Solemnly I placed a last bullet, the eleventh, behind an ear. Then we shook hands.

When we cut him up we found that the heart was shot to bits. Long before then the village folk arrived with their baskets, and by nightfall there was only a stain on the ground to show where the buffalo fell.

When The Ark opened in 1969 there were about a dozen old buffalo in the deep valley nearby. These lived in isolation or in twos and threes and very quickly accepted the building with all its noises and smells. We learned to recognise each one by the shape of the horns, mannerisms, and even the facial expression. They were the 'regulars' and we were the pub round the corner.

During the last few years buffalo have greatly increased on the Aberdares, in spite of continuous control work by the Forest Department, Game Department, and the staff of National Parks. This shooting does not, of course, take place within the park but in plantations, agricultural areas and in the adjacent hunting blocks. The population of buffalo on the whole mountain is thought to be nearly 4,000.

BONGO (*Boocercus eurycerus*) To choose the most beautiful antelope in Africa is about as difficult as trying to judge a 'Miss World' beauty contest. However, in the context of forest antelopes only, there is little doubt that the bongo holds pride of place.

There are two forms, the Western and the Eastern. The Western bongo is by far the most common and, in the great tropical rain-forests of the Congo, is still holding his own. The Eastern bongo, *Boocercus eurycerus isaaci*, is found only in Kenya, and even there in just four places—Mount Kenya, the Aberdare Mountains, the Cherenganis and the Mau. In the Aberdare Mountains alone, where protection is complete, can bongo be found in large herds and over fifty have been counted there together. It is probable that, like the elephant, when migrating over considerable distances, family parties band together.

The two races are similar but the Eastern bongo is bigger and has more massive horns. In appearance, the bongo have the same rather hunched up look of all true forest antelopes. The shoulders being lower than the haunch enables them to go under, rather than over, obstacles. They are as big as a pony; an old bull weighs up to 900lb. Bongos are coloured chestnut, with eleven or twelve vertical white stripes. Bulls, especially at high altitudes, tend to darken with age. Their horns, which may be over a yard in length, are an open spiral, smooth, with ivory-coloured tips. Both sexes are horned but those of the cows are much thinner, often nearly touching at the tips.

The bongo's food is, as yet, almost unknown. It grazes to a limited extent, especially during the dry season. Leaves, creepers and the flowering tips of various plants are basic, and they also eat bark and roots. The bongo's movements are a by-word and observations on the Aberdares tend to show that four days is the longest it will remain in one area. On the rare occasions when big herds have visited The Ark they have never been known to remain in the area the following night.

Bongo have one great weakness: when hunted with dogs they immediately take to water, usually in a little stream in a valley, where they stand at bay, grunting and stamping in the same manner as buffalo. This has made them a favourite prey of the

Wanderobo who, with their yellow dogs and poisoned arrows, have hunted bongo in the forests of Kenya for many centuries. It may well be that this has contributed to the phenomenal hearing powers, speed, and migratory habits of this animal. When running through dense bush, the big bulls habitually put their noses up and lay their huge, twisted horns over their backs. Eventually this habit causes a little bald patch to be worn away over the hips.

The first bongo to visit The Ark were solitary bulls. They never came nearer than 50yd and invariably bounded away at the first click of a camera. Today they come nearer, both single bulls and small groups. Yet even now, though they tolerate camera clicks, a carelessly opened window will cause them to vanish into the night. I know of no more dramatic experience than to be sitting in the viewing lounge of The Ark at, say, 2 am staring into an empty glade when suddenly a head pokes out of the leaves opposite. Twenty minutes may elapse before the bongo moves farther. Then it steps out. No painted horse ridden by the Red Indians of the West ever looked more vivid. No animal of the forest looks more beautiful.

Like the buffalo, the bongo's nocturnal habits are largely the result of constant persecution and when this ceases, as on the Aberdare Mountains, the tendency is to revert to daylight activities. With the bongo, however, this change is very much slower. Probably persecution caused it to take to the bamboo areas where the tangle of fallen stems made it impossible for a hunter to catch it unawares.

The bongo was only discovered in Kenya in 1902 from a single horn picked up at Eldama Ravine, an area where it is now extinct. It could well be that the great rinderpest epidemic of the 1890s decimated the bongo herds as well as those of the buffalo. Because of its secretive habits, migratory nature and forbidding type of habitat, it is not possible to give a fair estimate of bongo population on the Aberdares. Since the end of military operations in 1957, however, it has increased appreciably.

BUSHBUCK (*Tragelaphus scriptus*) Of the many races of bushbuck, the one found in Kenya is usually the Masai. The bushbuck is found everywhere in Africa south of the Sahara, apart from the true desert and the most dense type of the equatorial rain-forests—and of course those areas where man, in his greed, has exterminated the species. It is a typical forest and bush antelope, the size of a goat with a hunched appearance. Bushbuck are not gregarious, though bachelor groups up to four are by no means uncommon. They are extremely elegant with a dainty, nervous step, never relaxing their vigilance for a moment. Nevertheless they are a favourite prey of the leopard which takes them by lying in ambush in the type of cover they frequent.

All bushbuck have two peculiarities about the coat—a ridge of long hair along the back and a marked lack of hair in the form of a collar around the neck. This has given rise to a delightful legend among the Wakikuyu tribe. Bushbuck are notorious for the pugnacious nature of the males. Their sharply twisted horns make extremely efficient weapons and many dogs are killed during hunting. The Wakikuyu say that when Noah was trying to get a bushbuck into the Ark, a rope had to be used to lead him and this wore all the hair away.

Bushbuck does (or ewes as they are called in South Africa) do not carry horns, a factor which scientists cite to prove they are not related to the bongo. Yet in areas of mountainous terrain where bongo are, or were in the not so distant past, a very small percentage of bushbuck carry both the typical white tips to the horns peculiar to bongo and also the white chevron on the face.

The call of the bushbuck is a hoarse bark which denotes danger. In open ground the leopard is quite unable to rush an alerted bushbuck from more than 35yd, and in such circumstances it is by no means uncommon to watch a bushbuck repeatedly bark in the face of a crouching leopard. At each bark the underpart of the tail or 'flag' is exposed which undoubtedly helps other bushbuck in locating the danger.

Bushbuck are extremely common in the vicinity of The Ark. During the three years under review since it opened they have lost a great deal of their fear of vehicles going up and down the track. When the sun is not too hot they will lie close to the grassy verge and only get up when the vehicle is very close.

HARVEY'S RED DUIKER (*Cephalophus natalensis harveyi*) Of the many species of duiker this is the one most likely to be found in the forests of Kenya and the only one reported in the vicinity of The Ark. It is much smaller than the bushbuck, weighing no more than 40lb maximum. The duiker are much more uniform in colour and very much more secretive, feeding only in the early mornings and evenings. They never appear to become numerous, possibly because, being smaller than the bushbuck, the leopard finds them easier prey. Their warning cry is a shrill whistle.

When The Ark opened in 1969 a few Harvey's red duiker were seen almost every day. They have not been reported now for a long time. Besides being extremely shy duiker are very territorial. It may be that they objected to the presence of vehicles and man occupying The Ark and simply moved their territory over by a few hundred yards.

DEFASSA WATERBUCK (*Kobus defassa*) The waterbuck is not a true forest animal as it is level-backed. Yet waterbuck are extremely catholic in their choice of habitat, being found in every type of country from almost desert, stony hill-tops, thick thorn-bush, and semi-tropical rain-forest such as the Kakamega, Highland montane forest such as Mount Kenya and the open moorlands up to 12,oooft. In all these habitats the waterbuck must be able to reach water some time in the morning or evening.

The two well known species of Common and Defassa water-buck are very similar, apart from the buttock ring in the Common (*Kobus ellipsiprymnus*) and the white buttock patch of the Defassa. Scientists of the future may well classify them as one species as they interbreed freely in the Nairobi National Park where the range of the two meet. The species which is found all over the Aberdares is the Defassa.

Waterbuck are large, regal-looking animals about the size of a red deer, to which animal they bear a striking resemblance. Un-like bushbuck they are gregarious, herds up to twenty being common. Where their habitat includes lakes and rivers they will readily take to the water when hunted, and are powerful swim-mers. They will also take refuge in the depths of papyrus swamps where pursuit by predators is usually impossible.

Waterbuck are mostly grazers and feed at any time of the day or night. They are very fond of maize and, being heavy animals, damage a great deal more than they eat. The coat is long and shaggy and greasy to the touch. The skin exudes a strong odour from certain glands. Waterbuck meat is coarse, stringy and practically inedible, though the animal is preyed upon heavily by lions. The horns make a fine trophy and reach their greatest size in the Uganda race. Although a few waterbuck can be seen from time to time in the vicinity of The Ark they do not appear to like the area, probably because of the thick ground cover of thorny bush, Cassia, Sodom Apple, and Lion's Claw. This is most un-fortunate as these animals are a fine addition to any game-viewing lodge.

SUNI (*Nesotragus moschatus*) The suni is the smallest antelope in East Africa, the eland the largest. Both are found on the Aberdares but eland do not leave the moorlands. The suni is one of a group of forest antelopes which includes the Royal antelope (*Nesotragus pygmaeus*) of West Africa. Royal antelope are a mere 10in at the shoulders, the suni about 13in. Suni have a very limited distribution, being found only in the Highlands of Kenya, the Coastal strip and on a few islands near Zanzibar.

Suni are a uniform fawn to rufous colour, with the stomach and inner parts of the legs much paler. Their tiny horns are distinctly ringed throughout most of their length. They have facial glands which exude a strong smell of musk. These tiny animals are said to be silent but at The Ark, when leopards are about, they have been known to utter a shrill whistle of warning. Suni are extremely territorial: the pair which live amongst the Cassia bushes opposite the dining-room of The Ark do not appear ever to wander more than about 50yd away. They are rarely seen far from cover and are undoubtedly sometimes snatched up by predatory birds. When seeing a suni for the first time in the shade of the forest, guests at The Ark are often unable to grasp the fact that they are looking at an antelope, they think it is a rabbit.

GIANT FOREST-HOG (*Hylochaerus meinertzhageni*) This huge pig, the largest of all, was not known to science until 1904. There is no question that, with the protection given in recent years by the creation of the Mountain National Parks, it has now increased its numbers to the point where, in places, it has ousted both the bush-pig and the wart-hog. It is black all over and the long coarse hair can be made to stand almost erect, making the animal appear even bigger than it actually is. In the shade of a dense tropical forest such a sight can be really awe-inspiring.

The giant forest-hog is found in the Central African rainforests and also in parts of West Africa. In Kenya it has now disappeared from the Kakamega area through intensive African hunting but can still be found in small numbers at Nandi. In the mountain forests the hog enjoys better protection and is increasing. So savagely does it rip up the hunter's dogs that in some areas they are called off if less aggressive game is available.

The giant forest-hog's head is huge, supported by specially strong muscles. Around the nostrils protrudes a large disc of gristle. The extremely long skull has swollen excrescences in front of the eyes, flatter and much bigger than those on a wart-hog, which make it look even uglier. At the top of the skull is a circular depression about the size of an orange. The tusks are not as massive as in some wart-hogs but are razor sharp, and are used with a violent side-ways motion of the head. All old boars appear to carry a swelling in the pit of the stomach as though they are ruptured.

Giant forest-hogs go about in sounders from about half a dozen to as many as forty, though old boars can often be found alone. The young are uniform in colour, sometimes brown but often quite black. For the first few days they stay very much under their mother's stomach. So vast and low-slung is she that often only a row of tiny feet can be discerned, the one between her hind legs being more obvious as she retreats. First litters often consist of only two, but up to eleven have been recorded.

It would appear that these hogs have different habits in different kinds of habitats. In the dense tropical forests where there is little grass, they root a great deal, and no doubt eat berries and leaves. In the low country adjacent to cultivation they also raid crops. For this reason, many living near the Parc National in the former Belgian Congo had to be destroyed. In Kenya, however, where it is now confined to mountainous areas, the hog appears to be completely a grazer and there is little or no evidence of rooting. Indeed one old boar at The Ark habitually comes in shortly after dark and grazes his way all round the building, scarcely raising his head for perhaps four hours.

A giant forest-hog has been recorded as weighing 600lb,

though 500 is nearer the average. Even at 500 it is a lot of pork. At The Ark, leopards have been observed on more than one occasion stalking a giant forest-hog only to change their minds when they saw the size of their intended victim. Once there was the glorious sight of a leopard stalking a piglet only to be chased the full length of the glade by the old boar.

WART-HOG (*Phacochaerus aethiopicus*) The wart-hog is much better known than the giant forest-hog because, in addition to being much more common, it has day-time habits. It also has a preference for more open country. When feeding, the wart-hog goes down on its knees, on which there are special pads. When running it holds its tail stiffly erect. At all times it has a ludicrous appearance.

Although the wart-hog is found in almost pure desert habitats and is often extremely common on the grassy plains, it also lives in forests which are not too dense and is present in great numbers around both Treetops and The Ark. The ferocity with which the wart-hog fights all and sundry who interfere with him or the family unit is legendary. The warts from which it takes its name are excrescences of the skin, composed of gristle. They are not so flat as those on the forest-hog, being more conical in appearance. There is also a long flap of skin from the corner of the mouth which supports conspicuous white whiskers.

The tusks, or tushes, are often extremely long with the upper pair curling over the snout until they almost meet. The lower pair, by constant friction with the upper tusks, become razor-sharp. They are also straighter. These are the deadly weapons with which the wart-hog fights. Like all pigs, the head is swung sideways when delivering the blow. Wart-hogs tend with age to lose their hair much more than other pigs and sometimes become nearly bald. As they wallow so frequently, the body assumes the colour of the local soil. Although such redoubtable fighters, wart-hogs make delightful pets if the piglets are acquired young enough, and become extremely attached to their owners.

Wart-hogs usually live in enlarged burrows taken over from aardvarks. When these comical creatures, running with tail bolt upright like a flagstaff, reach this refuge, they do a smart about-turn and enter backwards to be in a fighting position if further pursued. The young are born in these burrows and, like the forest-hog, are a uniform colour. A big wart-hog will attain a weight of just over 200lb.

BUSH-PIG (*Potamochoerus porcus*) Although the bush-pig has not yet been seen at The Ark, it is certainly in the vicinity. Not many years ago I shot numbers of them at the nearby Kiandongoro Forest Station and they are sometimes seen at Treetops.

One day when I was at the Meru Forest Station in Kenya, the Forest Guard, Mtu Kanatha, burst in and said that a bush-pig was wandering along a path outside. I was inclined at first to tell him to run away, for not only was I busy but bush-pigs are nocturnal and shy animals. However 'Peter' was adamant and he never told lies, so I ran up to the house and took from the safe a Greener single-barrel shotgun and 0·22 rifle. I had run out of ammunition for the heavier rifle. Handing Peter the 0·22, loaded but with the safety catch on, I stalked down the path ahead, carrying my shotgun at the ready, with him just behind.

Sure enough, after a couple of hundred yards we came upon the pig, an old boar. One glance told me that he was suffering from rinderpest. There was an outbreak on Mount Kenya at that time and we had found a lot of dead animals. He was 30yd ahead. My shotgun was loaded with a charge of SSG, big pellets used for the control of monkeys and baboons. Upon receiving the charge he whipped around and came straight for us down the path. I rapidly operated the ejector. Alas, the cardboard of the cartridge had become swollen with recent rain, and it refused to

budge. There was no time to fiddle with it so I handed it backwards to Peter and took from him the 0·22 rifle. Sighting it on
the pig, which was now almost on top of us, I pulled the trigger.
There was a hollow metallic click. I quickly stepped off the path
into the extremely dense and thorny bush and 'guided' the pig
past me with the flat of my boot. It collapsed and promptly died
a few yards on.

Peter was also pressed well back into the bush. When I looked
to him for an explanation, he sheepishly opened the palm of his
left hand where nestled five rounds of 0·22 ammunition. 'When
you handed me the rifle,' he explained, 'I thought to myself, all
these years the bwana has been teaching the scouts that a safety
catch is not sufficient, the striking pin can sometimes jump. They
should carry a rifle with the bolt over the top of the ammunition
up to the time of action. So I pulled the bolt back a little to see,
intending to slide it back again over the top. But it just pulled a
round out, which I caught in my other hand. It did that five
times bwana, and I didn't have time to tell you about it before
we saw the pig on the path. . . !' Poor Peter. That was the only
mistake he ever made in all the years we were hunting together
and I had to laugh.

Taking Kenya as a whole the bush-pig is much the most
numerous of the three species and does great damage to crops.
It is smaller than either the forest-hog or wart-hog and is more
akin to the domestic pig. Bush-pigs attain a maximum weight of
150lb. In spite of its name it is primarily a forest animal and is
extremely shy and nocturnal; facts which make control of numbers extremely difficult. The colour of bush-pigs varies greatly
both in different parts of Africa and within the same area. In
West Africa it is replaced by the red river hog—in the Kakamega
forest of Kenya some of the pigs are quite red. Normally bush-
pigs are black with a white ridge along the spine.

On the Aberdares, the rapidly expanding population of forest-

Page 73 (above) Photographer Frank Lane with an injured elephant at the home of Bill Woodley, Aberdare National Park Warden; (below) The Referee: Ears spread in annoyance at the disturbance, this fine tusker comes to break up the wart-hogs' scrap

Page 74 Three widespread inhabitants of Kenya: *(above)* Kirk's Dik-Dik;
(below) Serval;
Page 75 *(opposite)* Greater Kudu

Page 76 *(above)* Lion asleep; *(below)* Leopard alert

hogs appears to account for declining numbers of bush-pigs. In other parts of the country they are still very numerous, especially in areas where leopards have been eliminated, and huge sums of money are spent every year trying to keep them in control.

Before describing the predatory animals that live near The Ark, mention must be made of lions. Two have been seen since it opened, but not close. A few inhabit the more mountainous parts of the forest and more are to be found on the moorlands. In some cases these are animals which have taken refuge there when the lands outside were taken over for cultivation. When shot they have proved to be no different from the normal lion of the plains. However, work done by Gandar Dower and others in the thirties proved quite convincingly that in the past a small species of spotted lion did indeed exist in these highland forests. The fact that all lions when young are spotted, and that the Wakikuyu tribe recognised a different animal living in the forest and called him 'marotzi', all support the theory. But no specimen of a spotted lion from the forest or the moorlands of either the Aberdares or Mount Kenya has ever been obtained since the shooting of the controversial specimen depicted in Dower's book *The Spotted Lion*.

LEOPARD (*Panthera pardus*) Leopards are found not only in Africa but also over much of Asia. In such a wide range of habitat it is inevitable that great variation exists and in size alone there may be a difference of 3ft between mature animals. The 'panthers' of Asia are now believed to be the same species as the leopards of Africa, but the snow leopard is not.

During the past few years the leopard population has declined drastically due to the great demand for skins. At present there is a strong movement towards the preservation of all the spotted cats and, should this succeed, there could be a great improvement.

The leopard is extremely adaptable and is quite happy in

virtually all habitats from dense forest to almost pure desert. It will eat almost anything, from mice and birds to quite large animals. Contrary to popular belief, the leopard is not fast over any distance and, should the intended victim detect it before the stalk gets to within about 30yd, the prey usually manages to escape. In the art of stalking and concealment, however, the leopard is unique. Fortunately for the human hunter it is a light-weight, and is often content with badly lacerating and then leaping quickly back into cover. Man-eaters in Africa are rare, but not so in Asia and cases have been recorded where over 200 victims have been taken by one killer.

A strange fact about the leopard is the taste is acquires for dogs when living in close proximity to man. So strong is this that there are plenty of instances where it has entered houses and taken its victim off the hearth rug.

Leopards at high altitudes tend to turn completely black, though usually the spots or rosettes can be detected when the skin is held up to the light. Such melanism is a genetic abnor-mality and is a development of the black pigment in the epidermis, hair and so on. Other animals also are affected, the trait being inherited and often seen within families. Melanistic leopards at high altitudes are numerous because of easier survival. They are better camouflaged in dark forest areas and mountain mists. Forest leopards are always richer coloured than those of the grassy plains.

The call of the leopard is neither a roar nor mewing, but a harsh sawing which has been aptly compared to a saw being pulled through a log. It also emits a series of coughs and grunts. When heard in the depths of the forest, the call is always very thrilling. A leopard has been known to weigh as much as 200lb but 140lb is more normal.

HYENA (*Crocuta crocuta*) Most people find the spotted hyena horrible both in looks and habits. Old books describe it as 'the undertaker of the wild'. Recent research has proved that the hyena, far from being a mere scavenger, only killing the very young or the very old, is capable of being a true predator. Hunting in packs at night, sometimes as many as forty strong, they are capable of pulling down animals as large as wildebeest. When hyena hunt like this there is no attempt at killing. They merely eat the meat bitten from the living animal and death follows quickly. When hyena hunt singly or in small groups their activities are confined to searching out the young or infirm. On farms they will often bite off the udders or rip out the stomachs of sleeping cows. Not until I worked at The Ark was I aware that they could do this to a buffalo. Late one night a buffalo cow was reported by the night-watchman as having been seen running across the glade with a red patch where the udders had been. A solitary hyena sauntered behind.

The voice of the hyena starts as a whooing bass, breaks into a falsetto, and fades away finally into a wail. The beast also emits a series of chuckles and squeaks.

Hyena pups are much darker coloured than adults. They are cute and playful. When adult they have jaws of greater bone-cracking capabilities than that of the lion himself. Full-grown hyenas are heavily built with huge shoulders and a sloping back. A big dog will reach as much as 160lb.

A lot of rubbish has been written about the sex life of the hyena. In fact their sex organs are extremely difficult to detect. There is an amusing story of a Kenya animal trader who sent a 'male' hyena to a zoo which subsequently produced a litter!

In the type of forest in which The Ark is situated, with more patches of dense bush than high forest, the hyena is undoubtedly the biggest predator, even taking young rhino. During the troubles between Somaliland and Kenya in the mid-sixties, when military operations produced a sudden glut of food for predators, followed by a dearth of wild animals, an unnaturally expanded population of hyenas resulted. Many Somalis, sleeping on the ground as is their wont, had their faces bitten off. Few survived such horrible disfiguration.

CLAWLESS OTTER (*Aonyx capensis*) Found in the mountain forest streams of Kenya, the handsome, clawless otters are big animals, up to 30lb in weight. Coloured black, they have a snow white stomach and chin. The otters have no webs to the feet and, as their name implies, no claws. Before the introduction of trout into these streams during the last half century there were no fish, so the otters lived mainly on fresh-water crabs and frogs. They often cause great damage in the trout breeding hatcheries, but it is doubtful if they ever catch many truly wild trout. Even on the banks of well-stocked rivers like the Chania, I have never found the bones of fish although an abundance of fresh-water crab remains as evidence of otter activities.

The nearest stream to The Ark is over half a mile away. Every few months a pair of otters arrive, stay about a week, and live exclusively on the frogs. One rainy season an otter chased a frog right up to the dungeon wall. The leaps became longer and longer as the otter closed in but they were of no avail and the frog was finally caught and eaten.

LARGE-SPOTTED GENET (*Genetta tigrina*) This endearing little animal is found all over the forested and bushy parts of Kenya. Often called the genet cat, it is not a true cat but a member of the civet family with the same type of scent glands beneath the tail. The spot markings are more like those of a jaguar and there is a distinct tuft of yellow hair beneath the eyes. The genet is a great killer of small roosting birds and raider of nests. It also kills rats, voles and mice. What people do not appreciate is the fact that it is also insectivorous.

A family of genets has been in residence ever since The Ark opened. They are extremely fond of the moths which flutter around the lights, eventually falling exhausted on to the grass. These are quickly pounced upon and the bodies consumed, the wings falling down each side of the mouth. The mother genet is extremely fond of raw eggs and is given a quota each night.

Genets hiss when approached too closely. When taken young they make excellent pets. A genet weighs about 4lb and is rather sinuous in shape. Like the leopard, a small number tend to go black and these melanistic animals are also more numerous at high altitudes where, like the leopards, their dark colour gives them a distinct advantage.

WHITE-TAILED MONGOOSE (*Ichneumia albicauda*) There are a number of different species of mongoose in Africa and this is one of the largest. It is very doubtful if any of them eat snakes as in Asia, that role being taken over by a number of specially adapted predatory birds. The white-tailed mongoose is quite common in all the forested and bush-covered areas of Kenya and is an exceedingly aggressive animal for its size, which is about 7lb. In a chicken run it will kill far more birds than it can possibly eat, but a lot of this killing may be a defensive reflex action brought about when birds collide with it in panic. It has a scurrying action, moving quite fast and trailing its big white tail behind it.

Like the genet, the mongoose is nocturnal and insectivorous as well as carnivorous. It cannot climb trees. It spends a lot of time finding grasshoppers and other insects and also eats many moths at The Ark, though I doubt if it ever finds many elsewhere. The mongoose assiduously turns over great heaps of elephant dung for the beetles and other insects beneath. Both the genet and the white-tailed mongoose have been observed chasing hares at night, but never with any success. The impression was that the hares, in their mad chasings of each other, went too close and sparked off a retaliatory reaction which had no hope of success in a straight run. Doubtless both predators do occasionally pounce on young hares, especially in bush cover.

BABOON (*Papio anubis neumanni*) This is the largest of the primates, other than man himself, to be found in Kenya. Baboons inhabit forests, bush-country, rocky ground and almost true desert. They do not appear to be wholly at home in forests, only climbing trees to sleep and as a place of refuge when attacked. They also descend from trees in a slow, painful fashion. Indeed, the old males often refuse to climb, even when chased by dogs, but prefer to fight it out on the ground. In mountainous country they sleep on rock ledges and in caves, always choosing those that cannot be approached readily from above or below.

Baboons are omnivorous, and will kill and eat young buck if they have the chance. Like elephants, they are fond of the moist centre parts of both sisal and prickly-pear, following quickly when the pachyderms have devastated these plants. Baboons are also very fond of scorpions and will spend hours turning over stones in search of them. They are adept at pulling out the tail containing the scorpion's sting before eating it.

In recent years a great deal of research has been carried out on the social life structure of baboon packs. There is a descending order of precedence, from the huge patriarch who leads and whose glance will make a subordinate cringe, to the youngsters who have just ceased riding on their mothers' backs.

Although the baboon has fangs which can inflict a fearful bite, it is not aggressive and usually avoids man. The intelligence of the baboon and the use to which it can put these fangs is aptly illustrated by a story told by a naturalist in South Africa. In the Drakensberg Mountains, a troop of baboons were climbing in a long line to their night's roosting place. A leopard was observed trailing them with the obvious intention of taking a youngster. Suddenly, as if by arrangement, two males broke away and went straight for the predator. One attacked from the front and was immediately killed. The other, however, leaped on to the leopard from behind and, sinking its long fangs into the base of the neck, killed it.

A whole book could be written about the behaviour of the baboons at Treetops. To watch them climbing methodically round the bedroom windows testing each and every one of the catches is an education. Baboons are not encouraged at The Ark, though seen often along the forest track. They are clever, but only when they are clever enough to wear nappies when they come aboard will we tolerate them.

A big dog baboon will weigh 60–70lb.

COMMON SYKES MONKEY (*Cercopithecus mitis kolbi*) This monkey is found all over the mountain forests of Kenya on the eastern side of the Rift Valley. Other species of monkey do exist in Kenya, especially at lower altitudes. The Common Sykes monkey is medium sized, with brown and black fur and a conspicuous white collar. Both this monkey and the baboons do great damage to crops. They also damage forest trees, especially plantations of cypress and pine, by eating the bast or under-bark. In areas removed from man and his plantations, however, they are a great asset. *Mitis*, incidentally, means gentle, and no doubt this is true. Common Sykes monkeys are usually caught by the locals in cages made from thin withies bound with strips of bark and baited with maize. Some tribes still eat monkeys but they are no longer as popular a diet as in former years.

COLOBUS MONKEY (*Colobus polykomos kikuyuensis*) Of all the Kenya monkeys the colobus is unquestionably the most beautiful. These thumbless primates have long, black-and-white silky coats and a bushy white tail. In this race the tail is much bushier than those of the Kakamega forest. Today they are strictly protected, as the colobus monkey is a leaf-eater—most other monkeys are fruit-eaters. In addition they keep very much to themselves in the depth of the forest. Capes made from their skins have always held a status symbol amongst chiefs and, at the time of Kenya's independence, a great number were killed and the skins worn by those seeking power. Today, fortunately, this killing is nothing like so great.

To watch a troop of these beautiful animals move in a long line through the tree tops is a wonderful sight. They will leap tremendous distances, one after another, never once losing their hold of the branch they land on. As they launch themselves into space the black-and-white silky coat spreads out like a mantle.

The call of all three species of primates is different. The baboon barks like a dog, and in rocky places the cry will echo and re-echo. The Sykes monkeys give a loud 'nyiou' followed by a series of whoofs. But the conversation of the colobus monkeys is something never likely to be forgotten. It takes place in the evenings and just before the dawn, and is a series of deep croakings which make the forest ring. Different troops answer each other from miles away. If one is close enough it is possible to hear the sneeze which always precedes the first croak. Both Sykes and colobus monkeys are rarely seen from The Ark because of the absence of big trees, but they are frequently seen from the track and often heard.

In my time I have shot a lot of animals, mostly on control work for the government, some by professional hunting, but I can take solace in the fact that I have never shot a colobus.

AFRICAN HARE (*Lepus capensis*) No description of the animals likely to be seen walking near The Ark would be complete without mentioning the hares which often give hours of amusement when other animals are absent. They are true hares, born above ground with the eyes open. They also have black tips to their ears. However, being smaller than their European cousins they are usually mistaken by visitors for rabbits. The African hare is nocturnal, rarely being seen more than an hour before dark. Their habit of wildly chasing each other, with the pursued jumping high into the air so that the pursuer passes below, is most marked just before the advent of the rains. Leopards often chase them but the hares' speed and jinking ability is such that not once have we seen one caught. Probably predatory birds, gliding in on silent wings, are more successful.

Hares do not fear even elephants, continuing to nibble grass until the trunk almost sweeps them aside. Then they will skip high into the air, circle, and continue from behind. They are never numerous; about half a dozen appear to occupy the larger glades in the forest. Nature maintains the balance by only allowing two youngsters, or leverets, at a time.

CHAPTER FIVE

Birds That Fly near The Ark

Of the many 'birds' flying near The Ark, unquestionably the most important is Park Warden Bill Woodley's single-engine Piper Super Cub. Bill swoops around most evenings just before dark and his dedicated work means that it is most unlikely that poaching gangs will be operating in the vicinity. One gang, using dogs and spears, could terrorise both beasts and birds, thus undoing all the confidence we are trying to build up. By flying just before dark, keen eyes can spot any trace of a camp fire. A radio message can quickly summon ground assistance.

Of 200 or more bird species we have recorded, 45 are described here and are likely to be seen by an observant guest at The Ark. Some, like the pennant-winged nightjar, are migrants of such short duration that they have been omitted, even though they may be spectacular. Of the others, many come in just for the breeding season, especially the water birds. Their family activities entertain our guests at a time of the year when the rain and the cold mist put game viewing at a low ebb.

CROWNED CRANE (*Balearica regulorum*) The emblem of Uganda, the crowned crane is numerous in the vicinity of Lake Victoria. A big bird, 40in tall, with long neck and legs, its predominant colours are black, white, chestnut and a beautiful slate grey. The crest is most conspicuous and the wattles a brilliant red and white. In flight the crane is extremely stately, neck and

86

legs being outstretched to the full. Its coming in to land is also spectacular.

The crane is distinguished by a particularly mournful cry. Believing that the spirits of long-departed ancestors are incarcerated in these birds, the Luo tribe will not touch them, even though huge flocks eat much newly-planted maize.

A group of beautiful cranes are to be found at the Country Club where they wander sedately round the grounds, providing an endless subject for photography. At The Ark, a pair have nested in the swamp every year, arriving usually in March and leaving in October. The male carries out a fantastic courtship dance which, if the visitor to The Ark is fortunate enough to witness, he will never forget.

Crowned cranes make very good parents, and like ostriches take turns incubating. When the rains are at their height and millions of moths dance around The Ark's lights, the adult birds bring their chicks close to the building to feast. They also spend a lot of time scratching in the grass to put up insects. The parents guard their young jealously, and have been observed chasing elephant, rhino, buffalo, forest-hog, leopard and hyena away from the chicks. They dance up to the intruder with wings outspread and, if that fails to scare them, readily take to the air to mob them. Eagles, however, appear to be a predator they are unable to cope with.

The Ark's crowned cranes have produced two chicks every year since they first arrived in 1970. The first year one chick was found dead after a particularly cold night, but the other survived and finally flew away. The second year both chicks were lost on successive days to a crowned eagle.

This year the family was just as unfortunate. When the two chicks were very small a solitary male hyena of huge proportions walked near. The cock bird danced up to him in the usual fashion, spreading his wings suddenly and uttering the raucous cry. The hyena, however, was either very hungry or just extra bold and was not intimidated. Seizing the crane by the neck he quickly ate it.

I am not an ornithologist and do not claim to understand the behaviour of crowned cranes. I only suspect that, like swans they mate for life. The hen bird continued to care for the two chicks. It was customary for the pair to take turns leaving them for spells of up to twenty minutes. She still carried on taking this exercise, only now she led them deep into the swamp first. She also started a cry every night which lasted the full three months it took the chicks to grow up and fly away. Whether it was a lament for the departed, a call for the old man to come back and take care of the offspring, or a call for a new mate I do not know.

YELLOW-BILLED STORK or **WOOD IBIS** (*Ibis ibis*)
Readily identified by its red head and huge yellow bill, this large bird does not breed near The Ark but comes in for long periods. When it catches a frog the stork washes it very thoroughly before swallowing, presumably to remove as much slime as possible. Besides catching frogs, it spends many hours searching through the mud for crustaceae.

GREY HERON (*Ardea cinerea*) Although there are no known heronries in the vicinity, the grey heron is often to be seen amongst the rushes by The Ark pool, especially during the rains. This heron will stand motionless in water for many hours, but when it eventually sees a frog it moves with remarkable speed. Unlike the yellow-billed stork, it does not appear to spend so much time washing its victim.

SQUACCO HERON (*Ardeola ralloides*) Found squatting among the rushes for long but erratic periods, is the small squacco heron, which is a uniform buff colour. The underside of the wings, however, are white and in its short, fluttering flight they become very conspicuous.

HAMMERKOP (*Scopus umbretta*) This is a dusky brown bird, rather larger than a duck and with a thick crest, which is often seen in the glade. It has a habit of following very close behind all the larger animals, especially buffalo, in order to feed on the insects disturbed by their feet. So far a nest has not been found but it could very well be in one of the nearby trees. The nest is a large structure, domed, and with a hole in the side facing water.

EGYPTIAN GOOSE (*Alopochen aegyptiacus*) A pair of rather small, brightly coloured Egyptian geese come to the glade every year and breed in the rushes. They have up to six goslings and do not appear to lose many to the numerous predators, running and hissing and honking at any intruder. When this happens to be a truculent elephant the geese find it necessary to take refuge in the water, but their courage always brings them back for another attempt at keeping the pachyderm away. One night a hyena went into the mud up to his shoulders in an attempt to seize a gosling, but failed. As with other birds, the moths form a great source of food, and late at night the goose will bring her brood close to the building. She herself never feeds but stands guard while the goslings chase around. Should a guest hear the honking of the geese in the night he is well advised to look out of a window: he may be lucky and see a leopard.

YELLOW-BILLED DUCK (*Anas undulata*) The duck most commonly seen at The Ark is the yellow-billed. Up to half a dozen pairs breed there every year. This medium-sized duck with brown, mottled plumage is distinguished by its yellow bill. Broods number up to a dozen but are quickly reduced in number and the mother is lucky if half reach maturity. One of the most

successful predators is unquestionably the white-tailed mongoose. They do not seem to mind the shallow water amongst the
rushes and a few can be spotted hunting every night from the
upper deck. The glitter of the eyes and the parabola movement
quickly gives them away. Like the geese, the ducks bring their
brood up to the building to feed on the moths late at night, and
they too stand guard. The story of how a mother saved one of the
ducklings from a genet is told in Chapter Seven.

RED-KNOBBED COOT (*Fulica cristata*) One or two pairs of
coot always nest at The Ark. They are heavy-built birds dis-
tinguishable by the red knob over the beak. These black water-
fowl are shy and only recently have they been observed approaching the building to feed on moths late at night.

MOORHEN (*Gallinula chloropus*) This is a smaller bird than the
coot, noisier and less timid. When skulking amongst the rushes
it jerks the tail with a fast, characteristic motion, revealing white
under-feathers. When leaving the water it trails the legs for
many yards, leaving a widening wake.

DABCHICK or LITTLE GREBE (*Poliocephalus ruficollis*)
Smaller again than the moorhen, the dabchick spends much of
its time diving and emerging again many yards away. Common
all over the country, wherever there is an appreciable stretch of
water, they utter a trilling sound which periodically sweeps
across, and conjures up pictures of blue water-lilies, bullrushes,
cool water and bright sunshine. All the grebes cover their eggs
with rotting vegetation before leaving the nest, the consequent
heat helping incubation.

COMMON SANDPIPER (*Tringa glareola*) These endearing
little birds with the bobbing head and jerking tail live around

The Ark all through the year. There is no record of them nesting in East Africa and it is assumed they are all non-breeding birds resting before returning to Europe. When The Ark first opened, a flock of about a dozen spent every night on the mud by the water's edge huddled together. Eventually they discovered the unending source of food provided by the moths falling bemused below the big lamps and have never roosted together since.

SCALY FRANCOLIN (*Francolinus squamatus*) This is the most common species of forest francolin, being found all over the country in both forest and heavy bush. The francolins are game birds, reminiscent of the European partridge. The scaly francolin, one of the smallest, is a uniform brown colour with conspicuous red legs and beak. Francolin are never found in flocks but in family parties of up to about ten. They are loth to fly until danger is very close. All francolin are noisy just before dark and in the early morning, their harsh rasping calls being a feature of many parts of the country.

JACKSON'S FRANCOLIN (*Francolinus jacksoni*) A much larger bird than the scaly, Jackson's francolin is found only in the mountainous parts of the country. On Mount Kenya and the Aberdares it is much the commoner of the two. Apart from size it can be distinguished by the speckled breast. With the elimination of building activity, the Jackson's francolin near The Ark have become very confident. They are often on the road when the vehicles are returning, and it is quite usual for them to stand on the grass verge only a couple of yards behind the stationary vehicles. Francolin have numerous enemies, and it is not uncommon to see a brood of a dozen chicks early in the season and watch them finally reduced to a single survivor.

HARLEQUIN QUAIL (*Coturnix delegorguei*) One of the

smallest of the game birds, about 6in long, this quail is beauti-
fully marked, the male having a chestnut throat patch, encircled in
white. It is common on the grasslands, especially at higher altitudes. During the rainy season, when this little bird is migrating,
large numbers pass The Ark during the night. Unfortunately,
many of them fail to detect the huge glass windows and fall
stunned to the ground. It is not unusual to have up to half a
dozen of them lying by the fire. Sometimes they recover. Sometimes they do not.

Around the shores of Lake Victoria, the Nyanza tribes were
wont to catch thousands of harlequin quail in cow-hair snares
set cunningly in the grass. The natives attracted the birds by
placing captive harlequins in little wicker baskets slung along a
pole stuck in the ground. At dawn they would chirrup like all of
their kind and so attract others to their doom. Fortunately, this
inhuman practice is dying out.

CROWNED HAWK EAGLE (*Stephanoaetus coronatus*) This
huge forest eagle is often called the monkey eagle and indeed is
not likely to be found in places where there are no longer monkeys left. Its size and crest make it unlikely to be mistaken for
any other bird of prey. One of the pleasing features about East
Africa is that, as yet the predatory birds have not been molested
by man, and it is not unusual to see eagles sitting quite placidly
by the roadside. As stated earlier, this is the eagle that killed both
chicks of the crowned crane at The Ark in 1971.

LONG CRESTED HAWK EAGLE (*Lophoaetus occipitalis*)
Although the names of the two hawk eagles are likely to cause con-
fusion they are quite different. The crowned eagle is about twice
the size of the long crested hawk eagle which is black with a long
crest. This latter eats rats and voles rather than birds. Rats and
voles do tremendous damage to plantations by eating the bark of

Page 93 With chestnut-red coats marked by vertical stripes, and curved, ivory-tipped horns, the bongo is one of the most beautiful of the antelopes. These very shy animals are rarely seen or photographed, but one night during Frank Lane's long stay, four came and remained for about half an hour

Page 94 (above) This photograph clearly shows what an ideal site was chosen for The Ark, deep in the Aberdare Forest; *(below)* a typical afternoon scene as guests arrive for their overnight stay

young trees, especially cypress and pines. The Forest Department gives full protection to this bird, and it is standard practice to erect hawk perches in newly planted areas devoid of such natural vantage points.

AUGUR BUZZARD (*Buteo rufofuscus*) One of the commonest predatory birds of the Kenya Highlands, this buzzard can often be seen, a grey and white shape, on the topmost branches of dead cedar trees. It is also one of the most likely birds to be seen sitting on telegraph poles. Like all buzzards it has a gliding flight, taking advantage of thermals. It is a killer of grass rats and rarely takes birds. An interesting feature of augur buzzards is that some of them are black. When in flight it can easily be recognised by the rufus colour of the underside of the tail.

SPECKLED PIGEON (*Columba guinea*) This heavily built pigeon, easily recognisable by its brown and white mottled feathers, is not a true forest species. A number of these birds quickly occupied the roof of The Ark and can be seen constantly. Others may be seen passing overhead.

RED-EYED DOVE (*Streptopelia semitorquata*) This, the largest of the doves living around The Ark, is a brownish-grey colour with a black half-collar on the back of the neck. It is often to be seen drinking at the little pool opposite the dungeon and one afternoon guests were entertained by the sight of an immature leopard stalking a group of these birds. Its characteristic *coo coo co co* may be heard throughout the day.

RED-CHESTED CUCKOO (*Cuculus solitarius*) This bird is common all over the wooded parts of the country, but is better known by its voice than by sight. It is called locally the 'rain bird'. The three notes, interpreted as 'It will rain', have a fierce note of urgency in their repetition which is most distracting. Once heard, the call is never likely to be forgotten. As most birds in Kenya nest when the rains start, the call may simply be associated with breeding.

WHITE-BROWED COUCAL (*Centropus superciliosus*) Chestnut-coloured birds with long, broad tails, coucals are heavily built and have a clumsy flight. In fact they appear to flounder, especially when landing from a bush on to the grass to secure some large insect, a common method of feeding.

The name given locally to the white-browed coucal is water-bottle bird, arising from the bubbly call which is reminiscent of water being poured from a bottle. Often in the evening this bird can be heard calling from the bushes of the valley near The Ark.

HARTLAUB'S TURACO (*Tauraco hartlaubi*) Of the eight species of turaco found in Kenya this is the only one recorded at The Ark. Common to all the Highland forests, it is a very beautiful bird, a mixture of metallic blue, green and red. The flight feathers are crimson, and as it flies from tree to tree with a long slow swoop, this glorious flash of red is usually the first indication of its presence. After alighting in a tree it runs along the branches with remarkable speed. It calls loudly whenever it sees an intruder and so is the bane of hunters.

RED-HEADED PARROT (*Poicephalus gulielmi*) This medium-sized parrot is common to all the Highland forests of Kenya. It is quite misnamed as it is green except for a small patch of red on the head, shoulders and edges of the wings. These parrots can be seen every evening at The Ark, flying over in flocks and uttering a series of typical sharp squawks. They are bound for their roosting places higher up the mountain. When the brown olives and other trees are fruiting near the building, the parrots come closer but they are always very shy.

CINNAMON-CHESTED BEE-EATER (*Melittophagus oreobates*) All the bee-eaters are vividly coloured. The cinnamon-chested is one of the largest (8in) and the general impression is of a bright green bird with rufous underparts. A true forest species, it can often be seen from the catwalk of The Ark among the Cassia bushes.

SILVERY-CHEEKED HORNBILL (*Bycanistes brevis*) This hornbill is common to all the Kenyan forests apart from Western Kenya, where it is replaced by the black- and white-casqued. Like the red-headed parrot, it is most noticeable when the brown olive trees are heavy with fruit. Whole flocks will then descend on one tree, staying there for days until it is virtually stripped. Brown olive trees are very common around the Country Club and there are also a number in the vicinity of The Ark.

The silvery-cheeked hornbill is a big black-and-white bird with a huge and grotesque casqued bill. It is extremely raucous and the loud calls draw attention to its whereabouts. The flight of the hornbill is peculiar, about half a dozen rapid wing beats and then a long glide. Hornbills are omnivorous. Besides eating fruit they often pull fledglings out of their nests. As if to make certain that no other bird can do that to them, the brooding female hornbill is walled into her nesting hole with clay and is fed by the male through a small opening.

CAPE GRASS OWL (*Tyto capensis*) This is the owl which is often seen squatting on the muddy ground outside the dungeon of The Ark, looking like an amusing doll, and taking off periodically to pursue moths. It is closely related to the African barn owl but is rarer and can be distinguished by the blackish-brown underparts.

ABYSSINIAN NIGHTJAR (*Caprimulgus poliocephalus*) Of all the sounds of the African night I think the call of the Abyssinian nightjar is the most nostalgic. It is a long, wavering, haunting sound. Although the bird is found in many other places, this call always reminds me of the cold open moorlands of Mount Kenya; of elephant and buffalo, rhino and waterbuck. The nightjar is the owner of those ruby-red eyes seen at night on dirt roads by the light of a car. It remains squatting close to the earth until the last possible moment, when it flutters up and flies safely away. Once, when riding on the bonnet of a Land Rover, I leaned outwards and caught one in my hand.

SPECKLED MOUSEBIRD (*Colius striatus*) A small flock of these birds habitually take dust baths in front of the dungeon of The Ark. They can be recognised easily by their long tails and speckled head. The name mousebird comes from their colour and the habit of running mouse-like along branches. Also the long tail can often make them look like a mouse, especially on the ground. Mousebirds, or colies, are extremely destructive to fruit trees and are normally shot relentlessly. It is a pleasant change to watch them in a forest habitat where they are harmless to man.

GREATER HONEY-GUIDE (*Indicator indicator*) This plain brown bird with a lighter stomach is often seen near The Ark. As their name suggests, the honey-guides are remarkable in that they have acquired the habit of leading man to bees' nests, knowing full well that there will be sufficient honey left over to supply their own small needs. Normally their voice is a distinctive two-note call 'weet—eer' repeated constantly until it becomes monotonous. However, when leading to the bees' honey, this becomes an excited chattering.

YELLOW-VENTED BULBUL (*Pycnonotus xanthopygos*) This is a very common and confiding little bird, easily recognised by the blackish head with its slight crest and the yellow of the under tail-coverts. It eats moths and also seed put out on the concrete roof of the dungeon of The Ark. Bulbuls are great songsters and contribute appreciably to the wonderful dawn chorus.

WHITE-EYED SLATY FLYCATCHER (*Dioptrornis fischeri*) This is a slaty-grey bird the size of a sparrow, with a conspicuous white ring round the eyes. It is quite common and can be watched with ease. The abundance of moths has changed the flycatchers' diet and mode of life in as much as they can be watched hawking them in the glare of the big lamps all through the night.

OLIVE THRUSH (*Turdus olivaceus*) Often seen around The Ark, this very handsome thrush has upper parts of dark olive-brown, a bright rufous stomach, and orange legs and bill. During the breeding season the cock birds become very pugnacious and frequently peck repeatedly at their own reflection in glass.

ROBIN CHAT (*Cossypha caffra*) The nearest Kenya has to an English robin, this common little bird has a well-marked streak of white from the eye, an orange throat and chest, and a grey stomach. The robin chat keeps very much on the ground, and as it hops there is much fluting of the tail.

MOSQUE SWALLOW (*Hirundo senegalensis*) The mosque swallow is a migratory bird, prevalent around The Ark during the rainy season when there is an abundance of insects, but as yet it has not been reported breeding. It is a large swallow with the upper parts blue-black, a red-bronze rump, and the under-parts a pale rufous.

TROPICAL BOUBOU (*Laniarius aethiopicus*) A bird that skulks very much in the bushes, the boubou is usually located by its clear and bell-like call. Indeed it is sometimes called the bell-bird. The upperparts, wings and tail are a glossy black. The underparts are snow-white. When calling the throat swells with each note. Boubous move about in pairs and indulge in a very close duet, one giving three successive whistles and the mate answering instantly with a croaking note.

DOHERTY'S BUSH SHRIKE (*Telophorus dohertyi*) This bush shrike is the pride of The Ark. A pair have lived in the bush opposite the dungeon since it opened and have nested there. The shrike has a skulking nature and is not easy to see. However, it is well worth the time spent searching for it.

Doherty's bush shrike has a bright-green back, a crimson-red forehead and throat, a black gorget, and a yellow stomach. A local resident of the Kenya Highlands, it is by no means common.

BLACK-HEADED ORIOLE (*Oriolus larvatus*) The black-headed oriole is a bright yellow colour and the black of the head includes the throat. It is common all over the wooded areas of the country and can frequently be heard at The Ark. The liquid, melodious whistles are deep and rich.

BLUE-EARED GLOSSY STARLING (*Lamprocolius chaly-baeus*) Of the many species of starling in the country, some of them very beautiful, this is one of the most common. A thickset bird of metallic green colour, varying in certain lights, it has bright yellow eyes which are quite distinctive.

RED-BILLED OXPECKER (*Buphagus erythorhynchus*) This starling-like bird can be seen clinging to the backs and sides of most of the larger game animals. As they search for ticks and blood-sucking flies they clamber all over the animal, even into the ears. Besides fulfilling this useful role of relieving their host of biting insects, they also act as sentinel. A buffalo with 'tick birds' on his back is a very difficult beast to approach. Although rhinos are often accompanied by these birds, it is much rarer to see them on elephants.

KIKUYU WHITE-EYE (*Zosterops kikuyuensis*) Not to be confused with the white-eyed slaty flycatcher, this little bird is much smaller, is bright green above and yellow on the throat and breast. There is a conspicuous white ring around the eyes. It is very common and can usually be spotted at The Ark in the bushes opposite the open verandah.

BRONZY SUNBIRD (*Nectarinia kilimensis*) Of all the many species of sunbird recorded around The Ark this is perhaps the most numerous. Black, with long central tail feathers, it may be seen amongst the Cassia bushes around the catwalk.

EASTERN DOUBLE-COLLARED SUNBIRD (*Cinnyris mediocris*) This is one of the smallest of the sunbirds and is very beautiful. The males are a bright metallic green; the upper tail-coverts are blue; there is a blue band across the base of the throat, and a scarlet band across the chest. These birds are very fond of the nectar in the *Leonitis* or lion's paw, a spiky orange flower growing profusely near The Ark.

REICHENOW'S WEAVER (*Othyphantes reichenowi*) The weavers are confiding birds. There are a number of different species but this is one of the most common to be seen near The Ark. It may be recognised by its black back, golden head and breast and black patch encircling the eye. Weaver birds nest in colonies and take their name from the grass-woven nests hanging down from the tips of branches.

LONG-TAILED WIDOW-BIRD (*Coliuspasser progne*) One of the most striking of all African birds, the widow-bird is frequently seen in grasslands. It is black, with a neck ruff and bright red on the shoulder of the wings. The body is only about 5in long but the tail of the breeding male is 2ft. During the rains the tail becomes so heavy the bird can scarcely fly and is indeed often knocked down to obtain the ornamental feathers. The males indulge in a frenzied courtship dance.

STREAKY SEED-EATER (*Serinus striolatus*) This little finch is common all around The Ark and the surrounding country. Tawny-brown with darker streaks on the upper parts of the body, it may be frequently seen feeding on the birdseed put out on the concrete roof of the dungeon.

CHAPTER SIX

Animal Behaviour outside The Ark
First Year

A trained student of animal behaviour would find a virtually un-
tapped field for study at a place like The Ark. No hunter, however expert and keen he may be, can ever hope to stand 10ft from
a herd of elephants living a perfectly normal life. And even if, by
some miracle he succeeds, he will still be quite unable to observe
more than a fraction of their night activities.

After more than thirty years' work with animals I felt,
before going to The Ark, that maybe I knew a little about their
behaviour. But my previous experience paled into insignificance
before the vast opportunities which opened up to me then.

During the year deaths have been remarkably few, if one
ignores the rats and ducklings taken by the genets. Many incidents have occurred, however, which doubtless resulted in a kill
when the predators reached the end of the glade and were hidden
from sight by the all-enveloping bush.

Fights, too, have been infrequent, and little blood has been
lost. It is my firm belief that most of the fights resulting in death
which have been a feature of Treetops are the result of unnatural
congestion brought about by putting down salt. Perhaps in
years to come the same will happen at The Ark. On a smaller
scale the huge lights bring in millions of moths which then form
a new source of food for both birds and small mammals.

Births have never actually been witnessed from The Ark although babies have been brought to the dungeon when only a few hours old. In this respect it is well to remember that animal behaviour changes once man is no longer a predator. Both elephants and buffalo, in heavily hunted areas, nearly always leave the herd to calve, and the cow stays alone with the calf for many weeks.

As The Ark witnesses the eventual full spectrum of animal behaviour it is but natural that courtship and sex acts should be seen. The sight of a big bull elephant standing almost upright only a few yards from the open windows of the dungeon, is a sight never to be forgotten. It makes a man feel humble and an intruder.

In that spectrum of animal behaviour one colour is usually absent—that which stands for humour. The wild has no time for acting. It is a stage of life and death and the participants are deadly serious. The young play, as do young all over the world. But the adults must survive. They do not, however, live a life of perpetual fear, as some people appear to think. Fear is but the means whereby Nature ensures that only those best fitted survive. I suspect that, other than man, only the elephant has the first dim knowledge of death. Yet, just after this first year period an incident occurred which had in it all the elements of true humour.

A leopardess had produced two cubs again and, when they were nearly full grown, she put one hunting in the glade area and the other down in the valley. The one near the glade acquired the habit of hunting around The Ark nearly every night. Sometimes he was joined by his sister but not often. The staff called him 'Teddy Bear' for his long ears on a narrow face gave him a very bear-like appearance. Perhaps the pair did occasionally kill the odd grass rat, but on the whole their eager hunts brought no reward and no doubt their mother periodically fed them.

Eventually that would cease as her new family came along and they must either hunt successfully or die.

One night, when a full house was at dinner, Teddy Bear appeared before the dining-room, walking slowly, parallel to the building. Feeding in front of the dungeon was the sounder of 23 giant forest-hogs, containing at that time eleven piglets. When Teddy Bear reached the corner of the building the big boar spotted him and alerted the whole sounder which melted rapidly into the bushes. The boar then gave the young leopard a long disdainful look and waddled over to the little pool to drink, upending his vast bulk on the muddy brink.

Teddy Bear, using the dense little bush in front of the dungeon to make an unprofessional approach, was not aware of this quiet dispersal. His head poked round the corner to survey the scene. One could detect a look of utter surprise when he found all the piglets gone. He sat upright for a moment, then looked around and saw that big black posterior. Immediately he began a belly-to-ground stalk.

There could be little doubt that the hog was fully aware of this approach and, as the distance decreased, there was every sign of nervousness on the part of the inexperienced young leopard. Arriving but 6ft away Teddy Bear stopped for the last time. Then he took his weight on to his left paw and lifted the other into the air, pawing as would a cat before a dog. Immediately the huge pig started to back out of the mud and the leopard no longer hesitated. He fled. Teddy Bear needed those few yards start for the forest-hog meant business. He was grunting with rage, his little tail twitching with anger. His huge belly swung from side to side and his short legs moved like pistons. He followed the leopard past the lounge windows, past the bar, along the length of the dining-room, and back into the forest from whence he had come. And the building sounded to the merriment of sixty delighted people.

People often ask me why the artificial light does not disturb the animals. Provided their eyes are not hurt they accept it as a benevolent form of moonlight. They also accept human odours; the heavy smell of cooking and woodsmoke; the drone of the powerplant in the distance and the nearer hum of human conversation. They accept what they do not understand. But they know it does not hurt them and it is always in the same place.

I have kept a comprehensive diary of all unusual events witnessed outside The Ark since it opened in November 1969. They are, of course, only what I have seen myself. In a game-viewing lodge like this there are normally two Hunter Guides whose duties alternate. I am aware that many exciting events have taken place when I was not on duty. They were not recorded at the time and to try to do so now would result in inaccuracies.

An amount of editing has been necessary. Unless the diary was written up very quickly one tended to forget the correct sequence of events, but writing at 2 am does not encourage good English. Nevertheless the truth has been strictly adhered to at all times.

28 January 'Tonight a young bull elephant arrived alone. He came right up to the dungeon windows and, at a distance of about 15ft, displayed a great deal. This displaying—a form of annoyance—consisted of ears out, trunk up, shrill trumpeting and mincing steps forward. Then he would shake his head violently and move away. He walked round the building doing the same again opposite the bar and opposite the dining-room. After this he carried on round the glade, sometimes spending many minutes at points where the bush went back into smaller bays. He then left at the point where he entered.

'He was an "Askari"—Swahili for soldier—elephant, one who guards either the herd or an old retired bull. In a big herd there may be half a dozen such animals and they may range some miles ahead. An old bull may have one such companion or he may have up to three guards. There is no doubt that the young bulls learn quite a lot from these patriarchs. Sometimes they are bad-tempered. More often they are content to "see off" the intruder. Askari elephants should not be confused with the young teenagers who delight in chasing all and sundry from the vicinity. On the third night after this incident a small mixed herd of five elephants came into the glade and appeared to accept it, coming right up to the building without displaying. As I was not on duty that night I do not know for certain whether the askari was present.

'During these first three months of The Ark's operations virtually no elephants have been near and great concern has been felt by all. Various reasons have been put forward such as the open dungeon windows, smoke from the huge fireplace, cooking odours etc. However, the most likely cause is the fact that some of the sanitation pipes were found to be too small. Now that they have been replaced by the contractor our troubles may be over.'

19 February 'At 5 pm three old buffalo bulls were standing at the water's edge when a cow rhino and her baby came ambling towards them. As is usual with black rhino the baby was obediently in the rear. The buffalo gave ground slowly and reluctantly. Suddenly the baby, about three months old, left its mother and went over to the nearest bull. The bull hunched its back, lowered its head, and, as the two noses touched, tossed the baby back about 6ft. The little rhino recovered and went straight up to the second bull where the action was repeated. It did not go up to the third bull but ran back to the mother and stood close to her head for several minutes.'

This mixture of curiosity and aggression on the part of rhino calves is common and often gets them into trouble.

2 March 'At 11.45 pm tonight a fight was witnessed between two old buffalo bulls which lasted about fifteen minutes. It commenced with tail swishing and three complete circlings clockwise, after which they changed and went round twice anticlockwise. Then they locked horns. As the bulls were in front of the dungeon the noise was terrific. When one started to gain the upper hand a younger animal moved in and butted the stern of the loser which then broke free and was chased away. After this the victor turned upon the assistant and chased him also.'

Mock fights of this type, without blood flowing, are common and are the means by which a herd leader maintains his leadership. The losers respect the strength displayed. Another male joining in to butt the loser has been noted before. This is also a feature of giant forest-hog behaviour although the hogs do not push but charge at each other like true gladiators. When the skulls meet the crack can often be heard inside the soundproofed building, and the force often sends one hog down on its haunches. But the hogs are not serious. When he means business the forest-hog swings his head sideways. One swipe of his tusks can open up a dog from end to end.

20 March 'In the viewing lounge about thirty guests were sitting, drinking, talking, or just staring out into the glade. The time was 10 pm. By the floodlit water's edge six buffalo stood placidly grazing or wallowing. Suddenly four hyenas came loping out of the dense bush, passed in front of the now excited spectators and went on to the far side. As they neared cover a cow rhino stepped out and scattered them. She then continued on to chase the nearest buffalo for a hundred yards or so. In the light of subsequent events it would appear that this was her big mistake.

'At this stage a fifth hyena appeared following in the wake of the others, but found it difficult to get past the buffalo and had to change direction several times. The cow rhino then returned to the bushes. The last hyena had gone, the six buffalo started to graze or wallow again and peace reigned in the glade. One or two guests retired for the night.

'Suddenly the bush across the rush-fringed pool exploded with activity. At first it was thought that a wart-hog was running, surrounded by the pack of five hyenas, but as they neared, it was seen to be a baby rhino with a "pimple" horn just showing. Each time a hyena got in front the baby bowled it over, but twice others were seen to run in and bite at the rear. The milling group had just reached the muddy area on the right of the water when the first buffalo bull arrived, galloping fast. The spectators were now all standing ready to cheer. He waded straight in through the milling pack, lowered his head—and the baby was hurled for many yards, rolling over and over in the mud like a barrel. There he lay still.

'The bull then began chasing hyenas in a lunging, pent-up fury. It is easy to bestow upon animals emotions which they do not possess. Probably the buffalo would have treated any species other than his own in the same way, regardless of age. A viewer on the open deck reported later that he heard the impact and a shrill squeal. Doubtless the mother heard this too. At all events she burst out of cover at that moment, moving very fast indeed for such a large and heavily built animal. For a few moments it appeared that even now the pack would finish the baby off for, as fast as the old bull chased hyenas away, others were sneaking back for a quick snatch at the prostrate body.

'But the picture was now changing fast as other buffalo arrived upon the scene. The mother was standing over the body, pivoting continuously as she faced each hyena sneaking in. Even so she found it difficult and might have failed had not the buffalo kept up their chasing. At this point, three hyenas came very close to the building and lay down panting before resuming the attack. When the last hyena had been chased from the glade the baby was seen to be on its feet and no serious injury could be detected through powerful binoculars. Shortly after this both rhinos moved away, our last view being of two rounded posteriors melting into the bush.'

Whatever is said about the rhino its qualities as a mother have been proved over and over again. And when a cow is killed or dies the calf will protect the body for days against all intruders.

Next day I went over the scene with a representative of National Parks but there was no evidence of a dead calf. It was indeed lucky as hyena packs must account for quite a number of young rhinos.

24 March 'Tonight the pack of five hyenas were in again. One of them was running on three legs and looked extremely emaciated. Every time it came near the others they chased it away. It does not look as if it will survive.'

It would be interesting to know if the pack actually did finish it off, and if, being extremely hungry, they ate it. The one weakness about a game-viewing lodge in a dense forest is that there are so many questions which must go unanswered.

9 July 'A cow rhino came up to the dungeon tonight about 11 pm. One could see the red on her when she first entered the glade. She had been wounded on both buttocks in a truly shocking manner and about a square foot on each side had been pulled down like orange peel, exposing the raw flesh. In addition there were scores of claw marks on the sides and stomach making it look pimpled all over like a dressed chicken. The staff reported that she came in earlier in the day with a big calf and that there were no wounds on her then. They are pretty good at recognising the half dozen or so resident rhino and there is no reason to

Page 111 (above) Two 'debbies'—4gal petrol tins—of salt are put down daily to attract the animals; *(below)* the nightly ritual of pulling up the drawbridge separating The Ark from the catwalk

Page 112 (above) The Ark's lounge with its large log fire; *(below)* looking out from the dungeon, the massively-built viewing chamber at ground level

think that they would make a mistake. She browsed, drank, and horned the soil for salt and did not appear to be incapacitated or in any real pain. Provided the wounds do not fester she may recover. There seems little doubt that a pride of lions have stolen her calf. She must have put up a terrific fight. Although many lions are territorial, some are nomadic and wander great distances.'

20 July 'The rhino which came in eleven days ago badly wounded was in again tonight. She appears to be healing well and has been rolling in mud.'

2 September 'At 5 pm today seven giant forest-hogs came up the path leading from the valley; two sows, four piglets and a huge boar. The path near the summit was blocked by an old buffalo bull lying down snoozing in the westering sun. All the pigs veered round him carefully until it came the turn of the boar following up. He stopped in front of the old bull's buttocks, butted them smartly three times, then scurried hurriedly away to rejoin his sounder. The buffalo took not the slightest notice. To show just how relaxed he was, he later rolled over on his side making a pillow of one horn. And he did not even shake off the tick birds moving across his face.'

8 September 'Eighty-six elephants were in the glade tonight, among them a large old cow with two long-healed wounds on one side. A Canadian doctor in the party confirmed that they were consistent with old scars made by shrapnel.'

Since this was recorded, one or two other elephants have been seen with similar weals. One in particular is only half grown so it must have been a young calf at the time of the injury.

20 October 'After many nights of cold rain and poor game

counts, this was the first lovely hot afternoon. A female bush-buck, apparently about half-grown, started racing all over the glade, white tail showing and jumping almost as high as an impala. Her actions triggered off similar chasings amongst the calves in a nearby herd of buffalo until it looked like a circus.'

1 December 'About midnight, just after a herd of over fifty ele-phants had left the glade, two cows accompanied by a well-grown youngster, came out of the valley as a group. We then saw that the smaller cow had obviously just given birth a matter of hours before. Parts of the afterbirth hung down and the inside of her right hind leg was red. The big old cow must have acted as mid-wife. The group stayed in front of the dungeon windows for about half an hour. During most of that time they screened the baby very effectively. It was weak, on tottering legs, with ribs showing. It was a strange pale colour and its rather pinkish ears were clapped tight to the body. The sound of suckling was once clearly heard. When they moved off, leaving a pool of blood about a foot across, the baby was right under the mother's stomach.'

19 December 'Two African hares were chasing each other around the glade when their frolics carried them right on top of a white-tailed mongoose busy turning over elephant droppings in its eternal quest for insects. The mongoose immediately started to pursue one of them. A hare can run extremely fast but so can a mongoose when it really wants to and the gap quickly closed. The chase carried them right up to the open verandah. By then the hare was only about five paces ahead but as soon as the hare reached the bushes the mongoose gave up.'

Unless a mongoose can pounce on an unsuspecting hare I don't think it will normally try to catch one. In this case the hare ran unsuspecting into the mongoose and provoked the attack.

A hare can jink so effectively that a predator finds it hard to catch.

25 December 'This morning was as beautiful as any, and there are many beautiful mornings at this time of the year. The snow-covered peaks of Mount Kenya stood out clear in the sun. As we came to the top of the hill, two waterbuck stood in the middle of the track. Between them was a newborn baby, still quite weak on its feet. The bull has been coming to The Ark alone ever since it first opened. We know him well, but for a long time he was very shy.

'Waterbuck are gregarious, normally living in herds of up to twenty or more. This means that, like the buffalo, a number of the bulls must lead a solitary life or belong to small bachelor groups. About six months ago it was noticed that a female had joined him. When they both first came close to The Ark it was she who walked boldly up without any signs of fear. It was very interesting to see how this gave the bull confidence and soon he too was coming quite near.'

CHAPTER SEVEN

Animal Behaviour outside The Ark Second Year

During the second year a great change came over The Ark. Not only did animals visit the salt-lick in greatly increased numbers, but their behaviour changed also. Now they took the building and all that it contained for granted. Buffalo would still stand for many minutes staring upwards but they did not wheel round and gallop out. Bongo learned to tolerate the click of a camera. They flinched and often raised a head, but did not run away. Elephants no longer demonstrated against the building. Most noticeable of all was the way leopards started to hunt all round the perimeter of the glade, even taking a short cut under The Ark when it suited their purpose.

On the track, bushbuck became used to the constant stream of vehicles. No longer did they dash away the moment the convoy rounded a bend. Often they would lie out in the open until the first vehicle actually stopped opposite them. Even the shy forest-hog sounders allowed the vehicles to approach quite close.

During the heavy rains, the number of moths before The Ark's lights was so great that often it was almost impossible to watch the animals for the fluttering bodies. Gradually, as more and more birds became aware of this vast source of food, a state of balance was created. Today there is a greatly increased bird population and their whole life is centred around the night activities.

The moths are still there, and some of the species are large and very beautiful, but they are in greatly decreased numbers.

6 January 'At 8.30 pm a big hyena passed the viewing lounge, dragging a bushbuck ewe. The stomach appeared to have been ripped out, as the body was buckled up. Following at about 30yd came three more hyenas. One of these was promptly chased into the bushes by a giant forest-hog boar and a few moments later another was chased by a buffalo. The first hyena reached the centre of the glade where it dropped the buck and commenced to feed. Nine hyenas then came in from the far side of the glade and soon all thirteen were milling around. Buffalo bulls continually chased them but the chasing was heavy and ponderous and the hyenas had little difficulty in dodging and then doubling back. Perhaps the four hyenas had killed the ewe when she was lambing, and the leader had carried off the body whilst the others fought over the entrails. The other pack would probably be drawn in by scent. I think these four are the survivors of the five-strong pack which tried to kill the baby rhino.'

12 January 'About an hour after the last of the guests left this morning the staff heard a loud bleating in the valley. They rushed to the open deck and saw, in the middle of a small patch of grass, a leopard lying on top of a bushbuck ewe. As soon as the buck ceased struggling it was dragged down the slope and into the cover of the bushes.'

20 January 'At 8.15 pm both the ordinary genet and the black melanistic were feeding on an egg thrown out to them from the open dungeon windows. The white-tailed mongoose then appeared, sending them both on to the cement dungeon roof where they watched it in safety whilst it ate their egg. After the mongoose had left the black genet spotted a grass rat at a distance of about

30yd. It shot down the dungeon walls, reached the rat in a few extremely rapid bounds, and took it almost without its moving.

'Only two genets were living near The Ark when it opened. These had two kittens in April in the dense bush opposite the viewing-lounge. One was the normal colour and the other black. Sometimes late at night they would poke their little faces out of cover. Only the black kitten lived. Later the genets had a second litter of two, again a normal and a black and this time both lived. Thus at the end of the two years under review there were at The Ark five genets. When the mother was once again pregnant, there were signs that she was driving them to new territory. If they came near she hissed and chased them.

'Of these five genets only the mother became passionately fond of raw eggs. She could be called up to the dungeon walls by the noise of a cracking egg and would sit there begging. The white could then be dribbled down on to her nose.'

21 January 'Tonight one of the four hyenas almost walked on top of the white-tailed mongoose as it was busy digging for insects or grubs in the grass. The mongoose jumped right up into the face of the hyena which stepped back smartly and the mongoose then went on its way.'

There may be something toxic or disagreeable in the flesh of a mongoose as there is reported to be in that of the crested rat. In another similar incident, a guest reported seeing this same mongoose stand its hair erect like a porcupine and again the hyena left it unharmed.

25 January 'Tonight a large herd of elephants with many babies arrived, and their usual antics before the dungeon delayed dinner. No sooner had soup been served, when a group of six young bulls came out of the valley along a path taking them very close to the dining-room windows. The elephants had been on a scrounging foray to the deep pit where the staff drop all the rubbish. They came like battleships, in line, with the leader carrying above his head a 4ft length of cardboard boxing. Waving it like a banner he marched on round the building and so to the salt in front of the dungeon.

'By now the rest of the herd had moved on so these teenagers had the place to themselves. The cardboard quickly disintegrated as they played with it and soon no more than a plate-sized piece remained. The leader took hold of this and flung it in the air. It landed upon his rump and for some little time he walked around with it. Then he stood and "shimmied" until it fell off. He moved a hind foot back until he found the piece and pressed it down. Then he put his trunk right back between his legs, pulled the piece out, and threw it disdainfully away.

'After this all six proceeded to the water where they indulged in a thorough bath, plastering themselves in mud from head to foot. Emerging, they started on a chasing spree round the whole glade. Rhino, buffalo, forest-hog and bushbuck were all chased with much trumpeting and ear-spreading. When the glade was quite empty they themselves formed up into battle line again and marched out.'

26 January 'A young male bushbuck was standing at the edge of the forest when a solitary hyena came out of the valley and started to chase it madly. The bushbuck gained appreciably but slowed down as it neared the end of the glade, where it was soon lost to view. The hyena followed the scent line accurately but, in the middle of the glade it stopped, sat upright like a dog, and howled for some time. The cry of a hyena cannot really be described as a howl, it is more like a banshee wail. Then it started off once more along the scent line. Possibly the howling was done as a form of intimidation, in the same way that lions roar. But more likely it was to bring up the rest of the pack.

These hyenas must not only be hungry but efficient predators to be able to kill such formidable prey as a young male bushbuck with its dagger-like horns. Bushbuck have a strong territorial sense, and no doubt this young animal would not go far before hiding, when the pack could conceivably get round him.'

4 February 'In the middle of a big herd of elephants tonight was a calf estimated to be little more than a week old. It tried to suckle. Not only was it an extremely small calf but it had a very big mother and the gap between its mouth and the teats was considerable. First it tried standing on its toes, then on its hind legs. Finally it reversed until its back pushed up against its mother's sloping stomach. At this the mother stretched herself out and so lowered the teats, enabling it to suckle.'

12 February 'At 10 pm the leopardess brought her two cubs out of the valley. They are now just over half grown and we have seen them a number of times. The cubs lay drinking side by side at the little pool just in front of the dungeon. A female bushbuck stood fully alerted some 30yd away. Drinking over, one of the cubs got up and left its mother who was now sitting upright watching the buck. The baby leopard did a belly-to-ground stalk but had only covered about half the distance when the buck barked loudly and bounded away. The cub then returned to its mother and drank again.

'Then it spotted a hare nibbling grass almost under the open verandah and set off on another stalk. This was much longer and the cub took its time. The hare did not appear to be aware of impending disaster and the cub came to within about ten paces. At this point the hare raced away without any sign that it had detected danger. Possibly it got the cub's scent. The cub's reaction was terribly slow. It chased after the hare but was soon left far behind.

'By now the second cub had also spotted a hare and set off stalking, but these efforts were just as fruitless. Nevertheless the two cubs carried on right round the glade stalking hare after hare, chasing them when they bolted until they were both quite exhausted. Through glasses one could watch the alerted hares sitting bolt upright watching. They allowed a cub to get quite close before dashing away. All this time the mother sat and watched. When they returned tired out she led them back down the valley.'

This was the first time that leopards had accepted the glade. From now on they came regularly—or as regular, as wild animal behaviour ever is. Before this they were so elusive that they were often gone before guests ever reached the viewing lounge.

22 *February* 'Tonight the black genet, now almost full grown, caught another grass rat. It had already eaten two eggs and so could not really be hungry. At first the rat took refuge in a small clump of bush around which the genet danced for some minutes until the rat eventually made a dash towards the thick wall of bush some 15yd further on. The genet had no trouble in overtaking it, and jumped around it continuously, allowing the rat to go only a yard or so at a time and making no attempt to catch it. It was snatched up just before it could reach cover.

'This playing with a victim is the first that I have ever witnessed in the wild. It convinces me that the cruelty shown by cats with mice is a product of civilisation and domestication. A wild predator is usually far too concerned in filling his belly. When leopards get into a sheep boma and kill so many, I am certain that it is a result of the terrified animals bumping into it and setting up a defensive reaction.'

9 *March* 'Late tonight I had cause to take a guest out of The Ark in a Land Rover. As I was coming back up the steep hill, a

giant forest-hog sow started to cross a few yards ahead and I pulled up. She had a litter of almost newborn piglets, like little black hedgehogs, under her stomach, which was extremely low slung so that all one could see clearly was a row of tiny feet. Only when she had crossed over was it possible to get a good view of the last one between her hind legs. How I wished I had taken along my camera and flash!'

17 March 'Tonight The Ark was visited by fifty-two elephants, the first herd arriving just before dark. When about thirty-five were standing in a loose-knit herd in front of the dungeon, the old buffalo with the square-cut dewlap decided to finish his mud bath. He is the buffalo who refuses to be intimidated when the young bull elephants go on a chasing spree. He just stands and glowers. The old buffalo emerged from his bath with great clods of mud hanging down from both horns, and decided his next port of call would be down in the valley. The fact that all these elephants stood in the way did not deter him in the least. He just plodded on, looking the warrior that he undoubtedly is. And the whole herd gave way. They opened up a lane for him. Perhaps he had done it all before, anyway they recognised and respected this fearless beast.'

22 March 'A big bull elephant came in alone tonight. While he was drinking at the little pool the genet came out and duly ate its egg which was tossed out of the open dungeon window. Then it crouched, as usual, up against the bush, waiting either for another egg, for the moths to tire and flop to the ground, or possibly just for the moon to rise. Eventually the old bull came up for the salt and soil only a matter of 20ft from where the genet crouched. The genet watched him closely but did not move. It was under 5lb and the elephant over five tons but that did not appear to perturb it. After a little while the elephant noticed the genet and displayed, with ears out. Then he stretched forth his trunk and blew. The genet landed involuntarily in the middle of the bush.'

27 March 'A sounder of giant forest-hogs came in after dark: a boar, a sow, and four piglets about six weeks old. They drank together at the little pool in front of the glass and, as usual, mother was on one side, father on the other and the piglets bunched up in the centre. One of the piglets came out of the scrum and tried to drink on the far side of father. The boar thumped it with the side of his head and it returned to the middle again. It did this a second time, was again thumped and returned. After drinking they all went back into the forest, mother leading, babies in the centre and father bringing up the rear. Discipline in the giant forest-hog sounders is always strict but seldom as severe as this.'

1 April 'Eight hyenas came in tonight. The pack consisted of three adults and five youngsters almost full grown but still showing the dark hairs of puppyhood. Our first intimation of their presence was when they surrounded a big heifer calf in a buffalo herd and we heard the commotion. For half an hour, just opposite the viewing lounge, we saw the fight going on. Hyena after hyena dived into the bush, we heard the bellows of pain from the calf, then an adult buffalo would come up and drive them out. Soon a number of old bulls in the valley heard the commotion and galloped up to join in this grim cloak and dagger business. Then the whole herd came out of the bushes and into the open to drink at the little pool, the pack circling at a respectful distance.

'The calf was close to the heels of a cow and we could see that it was dripping blood from both hocks and as far up as the tail. The herd and the extra bulls in the rear then proceeded to walk in a long line up the glade with not a single attack from the circling pack now that they were in the open.

'An hour later there was a great howling and the whole pack came streaming back along the glade chasing one of the young hyenas. They came to a halt opposite the glass, milled around for some minutes, then all lay down panting. One of the adults later got up, went over to this same youngster and attempted to bite its bottom. It jumped up quickly and the noisy pack again chased it back the length of the glade and so out of sight.

'It is impossible to explain all this fully. The pack may have killed, fed, and been indulging in a game. However, it is well known that hyenas hunt in highly disciplined and organised packs, whether searching for the living or the dead. They may have been punishing the youngster for infringement of their code.

'Certainly it seemed to me that the old buffalo bulls, by steering the calf safely out of the dense bush, had saved its life.

'The way that the hyena pack returned and finally lay down within the circle of The Ark's lights confirms my thinking that animals regard these lights as a benevolent form of moonlight. I once went out and tested them. The lights do not hurt even the human eye, and night animals have stronger retinas.

'At "Secret Valley", where leopards are allowed to be fed on meat wired to a platform because the lodge is not in a National Park, the lights are much stronger and are only switched on once the animal is feeding. Even so one leopard there invariably turns its back upon the audience once the large lamp is switched on, and would undoubtedly be off with the meat if it could.'

5 *April* 'Tonight the leopardess came in with her two cubs and spent about an hour hunting in the vicinity of The Ark. She was hunting to kill and her cubs were obviously being kept back deliberately. She lay down in the grass at the corner of the glade waiting for a buck to come along the path. Her cubs were many

yards back. Only a giant forest-hog boar arrived. The leopardess sank deep in the grass and allowed him to pass her at only a few paces.'

12 April 'One of the two leopard cubs came in alone tonight. The youngsters have now obviously left their mother. He stalked one hare after another on his stomach until eventually he was so tired that the hares allowed him to get really close. They would sit bolt upright, watching carefully, and not dash off until the very last moment.'

13 April 'At 5 am the leopardess came out of the neck of the glade and drank at the big waterhole. The glade was quite empty and had been so for more than an hour. Then she sat upright and "sawed". (Those who are familiar with the call of the leopard will know the two rasping notes, which have been described as similar to a saw being pulled through a log.) After a few minutes, one of the two cubs came racing up out of the valley and right under the open dungeon windows. It paused just long enough to stare into the faces above, one of which was mine, then it raced on and joined its mother some 40yd away. There was a tumultuous welcome with the cub standing on its hind legs, licking its mother's face and rubbing up against her side.

'One was struck by the fact that the youngster is considerably smaller than the mother. This fact is not so apparent when they are seen apart. The driving out of the young into the realities of the outside world must take place at a younger age than I thought. The scene was very touching and one had the feeling that one was a mere intruder.

'The sky was just lighting the snows on Mount Kenya in streamers of red. Francolin were greeting the new day with their usual harsh grating. Although it was cold in the dungeon nobody seemed to notice.

'After a few minutes of similar behaviour, the two leopards walked about 50yd away from the soft mud and on to the firmer ground near the white tussock grass which is so common to the moorlands of Kenya. The mother continued to saw, but now in a much softer key. Then she again sat upright and the youngster set off stalking and chasing hares. It did this twice but both attempts ended in failure.

'The cub then went and hid in the grass and the mother walked over to it, whereupon the cub sprang on to her head. This was repeated a number of times. One could not escape the conclusion that the softer mewing had been a conversation and that the instructions had been to stop this daft chasing and do a real ambush instead. Then the pair walked right out of the glade along the trail by which the mother had entered. She was leading.

'What happens before and after an animal comes within range of the big lamps is, of course, not known, but it would be nice to think that the mother was taking her hungry cub to a kill she had hidden up in a tree. The nightguard insists that both cubs are still living and that the other cub is now hunting on its own in some nearby glade.'

26 *April* 'Today was special for two reasons—a herd of bongo cows were observed in the valley, and the widely believed myth that leopards will not hunt in the rain was exploded.

'There were *no* guests for The Ark today. This has been the case more than once since the heavy rains broke. Rather than travel the 40 miles back to my home at Nanyuki I decided to go up alone. I could always sleep with the buffalo which at least are quiet company! I spent a long time watching game along the forest track and did not arrive until well after five o'clock. The staff greeted me with the news that the bongo had been there since 4 pm and that three leopards were harassing them. One leopard, they said, had been chased up a tree. I cannot, of course, confirm this, but six bongo were indeed facing a bush and some of them were making concerted rushes up to it, grunting much as a buffalo does.

'The grassy little patch was only about 30yd across and they all stayed in it until after 6 pm, when they moved away in a reluctant fashion. Perhaps there was a little calf in that bush, or it may be that the three leopards had been the mother and her two big cubs. A trio like that could very easily kill a young calf.

'At 6.45 pm—just before dark—a terrific storm broke which lasted most of the night. There was torrential rain, with almost continuous thunder. The glade was quite empty of animals. At 8.30 pm, when the storm was at its very worst, the big male leopard walked out of cover opposite the bar. He then walked un-hurriedly along the grass the length of the dining-room windows. A magnificent sight, the rain streaming off his coat, he then crossed in front of the tradesmen's double doors and returned close to the open verandah where he disappeared into the bush.

'Shortly afterwards the alarmed barking of a bushbuck rang out. There is no doubt that the leopard was hunting in earnest and that he hoped to take advantage of the storm by finding a bush-buck sheltering. It is quite true that a leopard will avoid wet whenever it can, and will not even lie on mud to drink if it can be avoided. However, if hungry enough it will obviously face the most inclement weather. It will also use it as an aid to hunting, as the lions in the Nairobi National Park now stalk behind the cover of visitors' cars.'

26 April 'At 3 am the nightguard awoke me and reported that the big male leopard was drinking. He did not drink long, as no doubt there is a lot of water around now that the rains are here. The leopard then walked towards the dungeon with a very slow and majestic walk, his skin rippling like silk. This male must be as big a specimen as possible, probably a full 9ft. He came steadily on and I was ready with the camera. At 8 or 9ft the tripod of the camera had to be tilted as he was so close, and focusing down quickly was not easy. At the first click he stopped, turned his head, and stared right into the open window, a stare that did not show a trace of fear. Then he moved unhurriedly on and finally down into the valley. One more picture was taken while he stood staring. Whether or not it proves to be in focus is not yet known, but the picture in the memory will remain clear-cut and in focus as long as I live.'

27 April 'After dark tonight a leopard started a long stalk in pursuit of a hare nibbling grass just off the verandah. One lady became so excited, exclaiming "It must not kill that poor little rabbit" that she had to be restrained from giving a warning. However, the hare proved to be quite capable of taking care of itself. The slight wind must have given the leopard away for the hare suddenly dashed off without looking round and the leopard, racing after it, missed by a foot as it reached cover.'

The Ark was closed during the month of May. This is usually the wettest month of all with few visitors. All the vehicles and machines were ready for a thorough overhaul and the staff were owed leave. The management decided that senior staff could spend the night of 1 May there together with up to five family or friends. No other staff would be on duty, so that cooking and food would have to be self-supplied. Bedding, however, was to be left for the one extra night. It was, of course, a party, with children enjoying themselves immensely. Elephants were already there in daylight when they arrived. The noise was such that nobody really expected game to come until late. Nothing did come, except the leopard which decided to walk under the building, then reappeared under their feet. A wise man never predicts what *all* animals will do.

Page 129 Standing momentarily on one leg, a crowned crane is caught with halo-like crest fully erect. Widespread throughout East Africa, these cranes are often seen at The Ark

Page 130 and Page 131 Cheetah studies. Nature's sprint champion, the cheetah can reach 60mph from a standing start in 2–3 seconds

Page 132 (*above*) One of the numerous herds of elephants that come within a few feet of The Ark's verandah; (*below*) buffaloes are also frequent visitors, by day and night

It is not expected that The Ark will ever close again as it is far too busy.

23 June 'Tonight guests were determined to miss nothing and some of them sat up the whole night. At 5.45 am the leopardess passed close to the dungeon on her way to the valley. She appeared to be in a great hurry. The reason was apparent at 6.30 am when she brought out of a dense bush two little cubs. She lay in the early morning sunshine and they scrambled all over her. One licked her face and the other eventually sat up on her back. This is her second litter of two since we opened.'

14 July 'The brood of nine yellow-billed ducks is now down to only seven. These are quite big. At 11 pm the mother duck brought them all up to the building to feed on the myriads of moths sinking exhausted on to the grass. As usual she stood back sentinel whilst they scurried about in front of her catching all they could. Suddenly one of the genets dashed out of cover, caught up one of the ducklings by the neck, and carried it back. At this the mother flew quacking to the water and the rest of the brood followed.

'In the bushes, the white-tailed mongoose filched the duckling from the genet. At 3 am the mother duck brought her surviving ducklings up once more. Again the genet dashed out of cover and was about to seize one when the old duck flew quacking over its head, and the beating wings drove it off. Then she flew on into the water and all the ducklings escaped. This is a case where a man-made attraction (light) provided an abundance of food (moths) and caused a wild bird to take unnecessary risks in order to feed its young.'

24 July 'At 10 pm a giant forest-hog boar was grazing opposite the bar when a hyena came along the bush edge. The hyena

H 133

immediately took cover and, minutes later, its face poked out of the bushes only a few yards from the hog, which was facing the other way. The hog continued to feed voraciously for many minutes, never once lifting its head. One could almost see the saliva drooling down the hyena's chin. Five hundred pounds of pork! Apparently the slight wind off the valley freshened. The boar stopped feeding, lifted its head and paused for a split second. The hyena did not wait.'

1 October 'When leading the convoy out of the Park this morning I was amazed to see four huge sets of elephant footprints coming *into* the Park. Eventually I pieced together the story.

'In the early part of the rainy season the Park Rangers reported that a herd of more than thirty elephants had left the Aberdare National Park and were heading for Mount Kenya. They had crossed the moat where a tributary of the Amboni river had weakened it.

'The elephants came back at the end of September, moving across open country during the hours of darkness and again smashing a way through the water barrier. Four old bulls, however, left the rest of the herd and decided to return along the trail of their ancestors. There were many small farms to pass through. The bulls moved in a long line in the middle of the night, no trumpeting, no belly rumblings, so silent that not even the dogs barked. Nobody knew they were there. Arriving at the barrier they had first to cross the moat over the "game grid", a series of wooden beams. Being old bulls their feet were broad enough to span these. Then came the locked double iron gates, 4ft high. The bulls simply strode over them, not waking the Rangers sleeping soundly in their beds 40yd away.

'If no human eyes saw those four huge pachyderms that dark, moonless night, the imagination can still complete the majestic, if pathetic, scene. Those four old bulls would be calves when

Africa was the Dark Continent. By their mother's side they had trotted every rainy season along a trail that was then only mud and grass, moving to a distant mountain in search of minerals and plants needed to keep the body healthy.'

10 October 'The old male leopard was sitting watching the little pool from his vantage point in the grass when a sounder of giant forest-hogs came in to drink. The family contained a huge boar, a young sow and another sow with a single piglet. As usual the piglet drank in the centre of the group. The leopard was no more than 25yd away but he never moved. He knew that he could do nothing against such opposition.

'Suddenly the female leopard appeared from the bushes to the right, spotted the hogs, and started a belly-to-ground stalk with the obvious intention of snatching the piglet. All the hogs had their backs towards her with their heads down, and the stalk went quite well until she was no more than 20yd away. Then a puff of wind from the valley betrayed her. Immediately the boar whirled around, grunting savagely, little tail swishing. Spotting the leopardess he charged and she fled towards the forest. He followed, and for many minutes we could hear his angry grunts and the crashings. Immediately the two sows closed around the piglet, keeping it close between them. Then they followed the boar into the forest. Throughout all this the male leopard sat upright and still, declining to interfere.'

11 October 'Tonight a guest threw a piece of paper over the verandah rail and it fluttered on the grass. The motion fascinated an old bushbuck ram who stood quite still watching it. As a result his back was towards the big male leopard again sitting upright in his favourite position across the salt-lick. The stalk was long and slow. Some of the guests said afterwards they were frightened that the click of a camera would break the spell that all were under. They held their breath as the distance decreased.

'Finally the leopard reached a grass tussock about a foot high and hid himself almost completely. What perfect camouflage should the buck look around! He was then only a yard or so beyond springing distance. At this point the night wind freshened. The buck did not even look round as he moved away and the leopard launched his attack a second too late, crashing into the bushes only a yard or so behind his intended victim. Immediately the buck's loud warning bark rang out.'

14 October 'At 8 pm tonight the female leopard walked in front of the viewing lounge and sat near a bush waiting. About twenty minutes later a family group of three bushbuck came up from the valley. The ewe was leading, followed closely by a half-grown lamb. The ram, a fine dark animal with good horns, was some dozen paces behind. Without any hesitation the ewe started to nibble the salt and the lamb joined her. The leopard, about 30yd farther on, sank low into the grass. The ram came up to the two but, instead of joining them feeding, he stared uneasily ahead. After a few moments, his suspicions being confirmed, he walked off into the bush without giving any visible warning and his family quickly followed. At this the leopard moved off in a line to intercept and was immediately lost to view.

'Nothing happened for about two minutes. Then the ewe came racing out followed closely by the lamb. They passed in front of the glass and out of sight. The ram then appeared in more stately bounds. Once clear of the bush he wheeled around. A few seconds later the head of the leopard poked out of cover about 15ft from him. Predator and prey stared at each other for a few seconds. Then the buck wheeled and raced very fast indeed after the ewe and lamb. Not until he had travelled some 40yd did he give vent to a series of loud barks. The leopard did not follow. There is no doubt whatever that she was within pouncing distance but that she respected those spear-like points of the buck's inclined horns all ready to thrust. And she knew when she was outmanoeuvred.'

5 November 'The big male leopard came in tonight and drank for many minutes at the little pool near the dungeon. A buffalo bull was drinking on the other side so that their noses were no more than 6ft apart. It was obvious that both were thirsty, for they took not the slightest notice of each other and, drinking over, went opposite ways.'

9 November 'This afternoon a sounder of four adult giant forest-hogs came in and drank and wallowed. They had with them no fewer than eleven piglets. These kept very close together, like a pack of little hedgehogs running on tiny feet. They appeared to be about a week old, around the age they leave the shelter of the ground underneath their mother's stomachs. It was impossible to say whether or not this was one litter.'

Later it was proved beyond reasonable doubt that they did in fact belong to one sow, as they were seen many times feeding. It would appear that first litters are usually only two but that the number in subsequent litters goes up considerably. Nevertheless this is the largest litter ever recorded at The Ark to date.

17 November 'During the early morning of the 15th an old buffalo cow became stuck in the mud at the big pool. This was the morning I came off duty. As she appeared unable to free herself, National Parks were informed. Ten men managed to get her out late in the afternoon. They need not have worried about having to run for it as she was by then quite unable to stand and collapsed on the edge of the glade.

'It was hoped that she would slowly recover. The first hyena coming up was driven off by shouting but it returned at 9 pm and made a determined attack on the cow's soft underparts. The predation of hyenas is never nice to watch. This one made off with a length of intestine. Nine other hyenas then came in. . . . It must be remembered that the cow would by now be in a deep state of shock and, in spite of all the bellowing, would be only dimly aware of suffering. They fed all that night.

'The next night a total of nine more hyenas came in and, at about 5 am, two leopards. I came on duty the following night and by then very little more than the rib cage remained. Within an hour of my arrival a solitary hyena came in, twisted off the last remaining leg with its odd pound of meat and made off into the forest with it. The staff all assured me that no vultures had been in on the kill. Vultures are not common in forest areas as most beasts die, or are killed, in dense cover, and leopards make great efforts to get their prey wedged in the fork of a tree. Thus it would appear that in just 48hr twenty hyenas and leopards had disposed of some 500lb of buffalo flesh. Some feasting!'

20 *November* 'Tonight thirty-one elephants were in and I watched one of the most amusing incidents ever. Amongst the herd was a big cow with three juveniles varying from about three months to perhaps eight years old. The family decided to snooze for half an hour at the top of the path leading into the valley. The cow stood lowest down the slope. Highest up the slope was the biggest juvenile of eight or so, lying flat on its side in the dust of the path. One could almost hear it snoring. Wedged between was the baby, followed by the next born of about four years old. The baby soon became restless and wanted to move, but it couldn't. There was bush on either side, a big prostrate brother in front and another behind. The baby got both feet up on to the stomach of the sleeping one after a great deal of difficulty but, each time it attempted to get a hind one to follow, it slipped

back off the hide. The second oldest also became tired and thought the back of baby made a fine resting place for its trunk. This pantomime went on for quite some time until the sleeper thought it high time to scramble up, whereupon they all came into the glade.'

2 December 'At 3.30 pm this afternoon guests were sitting in the viewing lounge awaiting the arrival of tea. In the centre of the glade was a rhino bull, and to the right a wart-hog sow and boar with a single piglet of maybe ten weeks. This sow first came into the glade with a family of three about a month ago.

'The rhino walked aggressively over to the pigs and they all ran towards The Ark. No sooner were they running than the big male leopard arose from the seepage-line which cuts across the glade just beyond this point and sat upright watching them. He had been lying there in ambush all the time. The wind, such as it was, came off the valley and so was in his favour. As the pigs ran he came stalking along the edge of the bushes.

'Arriving opposite the windows the family stopped and drank at the little pool. Quite unaware of the approaching leopard, the boar started to chase the sow which may or may not have been in season. The piglet was quickly left many yards away as the couple came close to the port side of the building. The leopard moved up quickly and the piglet, seeing its danger, ran into the bushes. Then the leopard pounced. Almost immediately there arose a shrill squealing which went on and on for a full, timed, three minutes. It cut into the silence of the viewing lounge like a knife, until it made guests put hands over ears.

'The boar was first into the bushes, quickly followed by the sow. His angry grunting could be heard above the squealing. There was a lot of bush-waving, and doubtless his aggression delayed the leopard in his work. One could imagine the scene below the bushes—one paw pinning down the struggling piglet, the other raised and holding off the angry parents, the snarls, the blazing eyes.

'At last the awful noise ceased. First out of the bushes was the sow, running around pathetically in circles. Then came the boar, a fine sight, with nose and tail up, loth to leave the dense bush where he had fought so desperately. That leopard is a full 9ft in length and wart-hogs must be very, very brave.

'A moment later the leopard was seen to glide across the path to the right of the thicket. In his mouth was all that was left of the piglet. He was looking for a tree with a nice fork in which to hang it. And the two lonely pigs ran back up the glade the way they had come.'

On this sad note these chapters of the first two years of animal behaviour at The Ark must close. During that time has been recorded births, antics of the very young, fights, courtship, death of the old, and now death of the young. For in the jungle there is no mercy and only one law—the price of failure is death.

CHAPTER EIGHT

Animal Behaviour outside The Ark
Third Year

Big changes have taken place during this last year. In the field of human activity work started on the expansion project to enlarge the lodge by reconstruction of the attic. The Ark will finally have 79 beds. This, of course, was only to be expected, but it does mark the end of an era. Another bus carrying 39 passengers was bought, and so we will no longer operate the fleet of small vehicles.

Greater numbers of buffalo visited the salt and caused concern. They are more destructive of habitat than elephant as they tend to stay in the vicinity. Certainly they are less interesting. During the spring, the resident pair of leopard again produced two cubs, and the antics of 'young Teddy' continued to entertain guests for many months. He left for new hunting grounds during the closing months of the year, and his going was a great loss. The following are further extracts from my diary.

3 January 'There is a very interesting sequel to the killing of the baby wart-hog by the male leopard on 2 December. A few days later the sow was observed accompanying another sow with a piglet much the same age as the one she had lost. All three came close to the building on numerous occasions and it was observed that both sows suckled the piglet quite indiscriminately, depending which was nearest. It will be remembered that the leopard took the last of the litter, and doubtless the mother would be full of milk. The fact that she became the companion of another sow with a single piglet much the same age would, I think, be purely coincidental.'

4 January 'During last month it was reported to National Parks by the hunter at Treetops that a very bad-tempered cow elephant had visited the salt-lick there, accompanied by a young calf. The hunter had noted a small wound in her side and eventually he had managed to observe her clearly through binoculars. A broken arrow head was seen, and the wound was slightly suppurating.

'This morning when we were leaving The Ark a herd of elephants blocked the road, forcing us to stop. A cow elephant charged to within a few yards, displaying and trumpeting a great deal. After a while she gave way with a very bad grace and allowed us to proceed. However, she had the last laugh. Rounding the corner we saw a big tree had been pushed over, completely blocking the road. All the men in the bus had to get out and heave and eventually we pulled it to one side. It is at times like this that one is glad that a rifle is carried.

'When the convoy of fresh tourists returned in the afternoon it was to find the road was again blocked by a herd of elephants. Sensing trouble I pulled over the leading Land Rover and waved on the bus. Again the cow charged very close. After the driver had revved his engine she moved off the road and stood on the grass verge. When the bus pulled up opposite, with rows of heads and cameras hanging out of every window, she stepped out, raised her trunk, and blasted a shrill trumpet at a very few feet indeed. The Hostess wisely insisted that the driver move on quickly and the convoy got through, although the last vehicle was chased. I was far too concerned to be able to see if she carried an arrow wound.'

22 January 'Tonight was very wet, with over an inch of rain. Forty-nine elephants came close to The Ark. Amongst them was an extremely young baby, estimated at no more than a few weeks, which started suckling right in front of the dungeon. The heavy rain quickly made a pool about 6in deep. As usual there was a great deal of jostling by the huge pachyderms and eventually the baby found itself pushed or dragged into this puddle. It was determined to carry on feeding and ended up sitting on its bottom with its front legs waving in the air *and it never once let go of the teat.*'

28 February 'This afternoon the convoy was at the top of the hill near the Park entrance when two young male bushbuck were observed, one on each side of the road. I pulled the Land Rover over to the side of the road on my right. The bushbuck stood with its back to the vehicle at a distance of about 15ft, taking no notice whatever but staring in a fascinated way into a low bush a few yards farther on. All at once we all saw, in this bush, the low-slung form of a large leopard. At this stage the leopard slunk away. Immediately the bushbuck recovered from its trance and bounded off. I have never seen such a happening before and it is interesting to conjecture what would have taken place had I seen the leopard earlier and stayed farther back.'

10 March 'At 7.45 pm tonight two young male bushbuck came walking about 20yd apart towards the dungeon. I was on the upper deck and, as it was obvious that they would come very close, I played the powerful photographic lamp down on them and then set off downstairs to inform the guests. When half-way, I heard a shout of "Leopard", so loud it would have done credit to a shout of "Goal" at a football match. It appeared that as soon as I left the deck a leopard dashed out of cover. He had timed everything to perfection. The buck had passed him at only a few paces. The wind from the valley was in his favour. One more bound and he would have landed on its back. At the shout he stopped in mid-stride, stared hard at the building for a full second, then slunk back into cover. And nearly fifty outraged guests wanted to strangle the now-so-contrite lady who had involuntarily shouted.'

14 March 'The nightguard reported that very late tonight a buffalo cow walked across the glade. Her udder had been bitten off and she was bleeding profusely. A solitary hyena came out of the bushes and followed at a respectable distance. I would have liked to know the end of the story but, of course, that is not possible. I know farmers often find their cows in this state but it is the first time that I have known it happen to a buffalo.'

17 March 'Once in a while we have a never-to-be-forgotten night. Tonight was one such. Elephant, rhino, buffalo and leopard all in together.

'The elephants were a herd of thirty-nine. Besides all their usual antics we had a trio of young bulls really putting on a show. They lay down, each with one leg in the air, and leaned against each other for minutes on end at forty-five degrees as though drunk, but actually taking short naps.

'The rhino pair were a cow and a young bull nearly as big as herself. She may have lost a previous baby and kept him with her for company. A big bull came near. There may have been a mating the day before. Certainly she would have nothing to do with him tonight. The cow and the youngster pivoted round side by side and faced him. There was plenty of puffing and snorting until the nose of the big bull and the cow actually touched, whereupon she gave him a sharp jab. He then broke away and galloped around in a full circle, passing in front of the dungeon, then stopped awhile to think about it, whilst uttering those ridiculous rhino squeaks. After this rodeo act he went off to hammer a bush to bits.

'Whilst the rhino was behaving as though it were in a circus, the big male leopard sat only 30yd away like a sphinx. He was not interested in rhino; only in the possibility of a bushbuck tripping past for his supper.'

28 April 'During dinner tonight one of the guests reported seeing a leopard for a moment in the bushes and that he was moving for'ard of The Ark. Immediately I got up and alerted the night-guard. From the viewing lounge I noticed a female bushbuck and a well-grown youngster at the little pool.

'A few minutes later the guard came in and told us that the leopard had been seen. I saw that the mother bushbuck had departed but that the big juvenile was still sucking salt from the mud. Its back was to the bushes and, twenty paces away, a young leopard we call "Teddy" was making for the path to the right in a typical stalking fashion. Sensing he was about to attempt a kill, I lined up my guests in anticipation, pointing out the place from where the attack would come.

'The attack was launched with dramatic speed. One moment the young buck was alone, the next the leopard had broken cover. The cat made two long pounces before the bushbuck realised its danger. Then, instead of bounding forward, the buck doubled back almost parallel to the line of attack. The leopard tried to hold it, both by mouth and claws, and for a second I thought it would succeed, but the buck broke free and bounded swiftly away. The leopard followed but could not overtake it and quickly gave up. I am certain that the buck was saved only by doubling back.'

1 May 'Elephants, in the mood for fun and games, have been around The Ark all afternoon. After dark, a small group came right up to the dungeon and discovered that the hole created by eating the earth made an ideal site for bottom-scratching. They sat on the grass with their huge backs to the open windows, put their feet in the hole, and then swung back and forth. The last couple to indulge were a huge mother and a calf about four years old. Side by side they scraped their hides on the grass, completely obscuring the view.'

25 May 'This evening there was a wonderful incident concerning old "Dewlap", the buffalo which fears nothing. We watched from the catwalk. A young Askari elephant was on his own. Probably the old man he guarded was farther down the valley. He saw a sounder of giant forest-hogs and went to chase them, but the hogs didn't wait. By the time the elephant reached the little grassy patch they were gone, so he looked around for something else and spotted the veteran buffalo. Ears out and trunk up he pranced over. Dewlap just stood and glowered upwards at the towering elephant. After a few moments the Askari turned away and the buffalo, no doubt thinking the place was a little unhealthy, moved to graze elsewhere. Immediately the elephant came rampaging back. Then old Dewlap charged. He caught the young elephant a whack on a hind leg as it turned. Dust could be seen to rise. The elephant trumpeted loudly and fled.'

1 July 'Our star genet has been on maternity leave. Last year she took just a few days off after one or two nights "on the tiles". This year she decided that, now The Ark was financially secure, nine would be more appropriate. During the tenth night she returned, looking more beautiful than ever, and decidedly slimmer. She ate quickly and ravenously. Then she decided that nine nights was not enough and took one more. Since then she has been in regularly but very late at night, and for a few minutes only. Presumably her maternal cares are pressing. If all goes well she will put her head out of the big bush late one night and beside her will be the faces of the new arrivals. It seems that the sole survivor of the last litter has now been driven away as we have not seen it for a long time.'

8 July 'Late tonight a buffalo cow came in with a yearling and a very young calf and stood in front of the dungeon. A solitary hyena came up and stood near. The cow lunged at him in the usual manner. He stepped smartly aside and returned, showing every sign of wanting to snatch at the calf. She again lunged at him and this continued two or three times. Suddenly the cow appeared to realise that the hyena was a serious threat to her calf. She plunged straight into the mud and water, taking her family with her. Floundering through she made off into the forest. The hyena could not follow and he made no effort to go the long way round. It would be interesting to know what kind of message she gave her two calves, but from the determined way they kept up with her I do not doubt that she did communicate with them.'

21 July 'The young leopard "Teddy Bear" has been in most nights lately and he gives tremendous entertainment to the guests. At dusk tonight he poked his head out of the bushes near the dungeon. At once a huge wart-hog some distance away spotted him. The mane along the back and shoulders of the hog stood on end and he started to prance over to see the leopard off. At this point the sister of young Teddy also emerged and the two leopards sat upright side by side. Seeing this the wart-hog changed his mind and fled. Both leopards then set off after him but in a very half-hearted fashion, making no effort to touch him, though very close. Had they done so I do not doubt he would have cut them up badly. I think they both knew it.'

147

17 August 'In the early evening and night 135 buffalo were counted in the glade. In such a huge herd there were obviously a number of breeding bulls. There were also a number of our old resident bulls around and soon it was obvious that there would be trouble. It was hard to be certain which bull was which but as far as I know one of the outsiders attacked one of the herd bulls. There was no circling as is the usual ritual in pushing-around bouts. This bull charged from about 30yd with no hesitation about it. The sound was not only clearly heard but the impact put the other buffalo down on his knees. The fight was furious but it did not last many minutes, and soon it was obvious that the herd bull was superior. He not only put the attacker to flight but chased him right out of the glade.

'Returning he then attacked another nearby bull. Again the charge was started from about 30yd, and again with such ferocity and power that the victim was forced on to his knees. This fight also only lasted a few minutes. The herd bull then attacked another in the same way. This time, however, the fight was much more even and lasted over twenty minutes. Both were obviously exhausted by the terrific energy expended. Eventually the herd bull broke free and fled. The new leader gave chase and administered one final thump in the buttocks. When he returned we could see blood on his boss and also on his chest. This is the first time that I have witnessed fights so serious, and also the first time I have seen a herd bull vanquished.'

18 August 'Tonight thirty-two elephants were in with a lot of babies. There was the usual family life activity. We see a lot of this, and I have known babies lie down just for the pleasure of being caressed by the adults, who used both trunk and feet. This time, however, I witnessed something never seen before in all my years of watching animals.

Page 149 (*above*) Spotted hyenas on the alert; (*below*) a sounder of giant forest-hogs pause to refresh themselves at a salt-lick

Page 150 (*above*) Young elephant poses for the camera near the dungeon
Page 151 (*opposite*) Ignoring the photographer, a male bushbuck grazes
placidly at The Orphanage

Page 152 (above) The wart-like protuberances clearly show how this hog got its name; (below) relic of a pre-historic age, the black rhinoceros. Those seen at The Ark are often 'red' through wallowing in the reddish-brown earth

'A youngster of about three years lay on his side outside the dungeon. A big cow came over and stood above him. Then she moved her legs in a bunched up fashion until she had him cradled. She lowered the stomach until she could finally rub it along his ribs. One could clearly hear the rasping noise made by the two hides. No human mother ever cradled her child and caressed it more effectively than did that cow elephant tonight.'

'Teddy Bear was in again tonight. He hunted first all around the building but caught nothing and was not seen again for some time. Then he was spotted sitting outside the bush opposite the verandah, interested in something far out in the marsh. The eye-sight of leopards at night is very keen. It was some minutes before we noted what he was watching. Through glasses we could see it was a marsh mongoose moving towards him.

'Teddy waited until the mongoose was about 20yd away, then he set off in long bounds. At once the mongoose turned and ran off as fast as it could, squeaking loudly all the time. The leopard overtook it in about a hundred yard's chase. Reaching it he made no effort to pick it up but danced around. Then he stopped and watched it go. The marsh mongoose is a fairly large animal, about 6lb in weight. Obviously the leopard was either not hungry or he did not fancy mongoose for his supper.'

29 *August* 'It would be wishful thinking to believe that no poaching takes place within this Park. There is, however, no large-scale poaching. The activities of hit-and-run weekend farm labour we will never be able to stop. Last night a giant forest-hog came in with a spear sticking out of its ribs and died near the building. I was not on duty. It was reported that only two hyenas found it before dawn. Tonight five came in. Soon there

was very little of the carcass left. With obviously full and sagging bellies they then indulged in a very noisy orchestral session. Besides the normal wailing there was chuckling, squeaks and diabolical laughing. No words of mine could describe the row. It is not often heard and may be associated with a full belly and the deep satisfaction which goes with it. After they had left, one returned and lay down on the grass in the full glare of the lights. He had his back to the building and his head on his paws. He lay thus for more than half an hour. It had been a hot day and probably the short-grazed grass felt nicer than the dew-soaked bush.'

25 September 'Today was one of my off-duty days but I had to go up to The Ark just before noon as Frank Lane, who is staying there to obtain photographs for this book, needed more film. On the return journey through the Park I rounded a corner and saw a huge troop of baboons spread out right across the road. There must have been more than fifty, of every size possible. In the midst of them was a solitary female bushbuck, standing quite still. Almost at her feet lay a dead fawn, perhaps a week old. Four baboons were tearing at the body. As I drew near a big dog baboon picked the dead fawn up and ran away with it, the legs trailing on the ground. The rest of the pack dispersed, together with the bushbuck. This is the first time I have witnessed such a thing. Doubtless the pack surrounded the pair before the mother realised the danger.

'A feature of this incident is that when the big bus and the guests returned a few hours later they found the bushbuck in the same place, still standing in a state of shock. Most of the baboons had gone, doubtless having eaten all the remnants of the fawn. However, two were quite close to the mother, and they were making tentative reaches towards her. Unless she recovered quickly they would kill her as well.'

29 September 'Three times now we have had a baby rhino in. It comes quite alone late at night when the glade is empty and stays on the salt a long time, eating the earth ravenously. As this is contrary to normal rhino behaviour we must assume that it is lacking in salt requirement now that it is no longer obtaining its mother's milk. It is around ten months old and has a pimple horn just showing. It must be about three months since we first saw it. Whether its mother has been killed by poachers we do not know. A pride of lions would surely have killed them both. Most likely a heavy cable snare killed her.

'When the youngster was in tonight old "Scarface" arrived. This is the rhino bull with the jabs all over his face acquired during recent love-making. He immediately chased the baby which ran as fast as it could into the bush. From the determined nature of the chasing I am quite certain the baby would have been killed had it been overtaken. About twenty minutes later it again came on to the salt, and was again chased. Sometime later, when old Scarface had left, the baby again appeared. It was extremely nervous and, when a group of buffalo came near, it fled for the third time. It did not return. A baby rhino was once killed at Treetops by an old bull whose attentions were no longer acceptable to the cow and this would seem to be characteristic behaviour of rhino bulls.'

30 September 'This was certainly a hyena night. At 7.30 pm a herd of over forty buffalo started to leave the glade in a long line, when two hyena suddenly appeared and singled out a calf of about eleven months. They drove the calf into dense bush, and the mother turned to defend it. The rest of the herd carried on.

'For the next half hour a raging battle could be clearly heard: the calf's bellows of pain, the grunts of the mother, and crashings in the dense bush. During this time nine more hyena came loping across the glade and joined in.

'The fight then moved much closer to The Ark, its passage being marked by the continuous noise and the waving bush. A stand was made near the glassed-in viewing lounge. From time to time a hyena came out of the bush and howled. Eventually this was answered and a second pack of thirteen appeared at the end of the glade. Immediately half the first pack came out of the bushes and raced to greet them, stubby tails held high.

'Meanwhile a number of the old resident bulls came from the valley and joined in. Twice the milling animals came into view and we could see the calf clearly. Its tail was completely bitten off, a section of meat was missing from just below, and there were numerous wounds right down to the hocks. It followed close behind its mother.

'The fight settled down. Sometimes as many as six hyenas could be seen resting, with heads on paws. Twenty-five hyenas, nine buffalo bulls and the mother appeared to be involved. From time to time hyena would dance right up to the lowered head of one of the bulls but they were rarely tempted to move more than a few paces in retaliation. Nevertheless renewed bellowings always indicated that other hyenas were breaking through the cordon.

'About midnight, four and a half hours after the start of the fight, the bellowing ceased, and shortly after this the nine bulls came into the open and dispersed. Probably one was the herd bull but this could not be confirmed. The cow doubtless remained with her dead calf.

'The periodic howlings of the hyenas now changed to the cacklings, squeaks, and diabolic laughs associated with feeding. Soon a few of the animals came out of the bush carrying torn off legs and belly parts.

'At 4 am a couple of hyenas came out of the bush to drink at the nearby pool. A solitary giant forest-hog already there charged them but quickly changed his mind when he saw more hyenas appearing and fled. Eventually all the hyenas came and drank deeply. By dawn the glade was empty.

'Many guests were distressed at witnessing this drama of the wild and retired early. One lady, however, watched the whole night through. Next morning she was as if shell-shocked, talking in a flat hushed voice.'

As is usual after a big kill, game-viewing at The Ark the following night was poor. Only a few pounds of gut remained. The intrepid giant forest-hog boar came along about 7.30 pm and ate half of it, and at midnight a leopard ran off with the remainder. A few hyenas roamed the glade but other animals with young kept away for the smell of death still hung heavy on the air.

CHAPTER NINE

Human Behaviour inside The Ark

It was not easy for one who had spent most of his life among animals in lonely places to fit in with the requirements of a modern game-viewing lodge. It took a great deal of willpower to acquire that party spirit so necessary to a good host, and to make the nights go with a swing.

I divided all my guests into two simple categories—ordinary people, like myself, and the afflicted ones. The afflicted ones included VIPs, the aged and the infirm. How apprehensive I was when told there were VIPs. The aged and the infirm I took tremendous pleasure in caring for. The ordinary people just swam with the tide. And what a tide! I suppose my bald head and my rifle feature in thousands of photographs all over the world. One I know shows a young lady with both hands gripping my neck in a stranglehold and kissing my cheek. 'Just a picture to show me saying farewell to the hunter' she called it. To make matters worse the photographer took five minutes to get everything ready. And then her friend said she would like a picture like that too!

One day I was told that Lord and Lady Blank were spending a night at The Ark and must be given special treatment. They were to travel in my Land Rover together with their ten-year-old son who sat on the front seat. We were, of course, leading the convoy. The boy pulled out a comic and sat engrossed in it throughout the four and a half miles of forest track, even when his mother repeatedly said: 'Darling do look at that big water buffalo' or: 'Darling do look at that pretty little deer.'

The Ark was not officially opened until 25 November 1970, rather more than one year after it had been first opened to the general public. The reason for the delay was that the altitude had precluded the President from officiating, and that Mama Ngina, his wife, had been touring America. Finally the Minister for Tourism and Wildlife performed the ceremony. On the 24th the professional photographer, Mr Dhillan, of Nairobi, was due to arrive at the Country Club to cover the ceremony. At 11 am a radio message told us that about fifty elephants were marching into the glade. Dhillan arrived a few minutes later and was quickly bundled into a Land Rover, together with all his equipment.

Arriving at The Ark about half an hour later I found elephants all around the building. The sun was right and the wind, coming off the valley, made prospects of photography in the centre of the glade ideal. The only difficulty was the fact that a herd of some twenty buffalo stood exactly where we wanted to be. I went out alone with my rifle and eventually succeeded in moving them away, without disturbing the great pachyderms. Then I escorted Mr Dhillan out, and sat him in the centre of the glade, together with his great mass of equipment, and crouched beside him. I had the rifle loaded, and I prayed that I would not have to use it. He took hundreds of feet of cine film in black and white, and many still pictures, showing elephants all round the building.

During this time two late-arriving elephants passed within twenty paces of us but we both sat very still and our luck held, for we remained undetected. Mr Dhillan had worked as a freelance photographer during the Congo troubles. He did not give the elephants more than a passing glance, but carried on efficiently the moment I whispered they were beyond hearing. He was just changing to colour when the whole herd decided, without warning, to move off to the valley. Those pictures were the making of The Ark and were shown all over the world. We had waited for just over a year. When The Ark was officially opened next day no elephants came near.

In the early months of The Ark a number of professional photographers and publicity people came with the intention of obtaining first-class pictures of elephants outside the building. National Parks co-operated by making hides and providing an armed escort. Usually they stayed about three days—and usually the elephants arrived on the fourth!

One photographer had a hide built about 100yd from the building. He was escorted to it before the arrival of the guests and there he sat waiting for the great moment. His spare camera lenses and other pieces of equipment were in a little woven basket which he hung up in the bushes for safety. Unfortunately there was a red band round this basket which could be seen through binoculars.

About 4 pm guests started asking me what species of red bird was sitting in the bushes across the glade. For some while I succeeded in stalling, but the question was asked with disturbing frequency. So, with a flash of inspiration, I replied: 'Oh that. It's the Red-Bellied Go-Away-Bird.' When I saw a guest with John Williams's book, *A Field Guide to the Birds of East and Central Africa* (Collins) open at the page 'White-Bellied Go-Away-Bird', I thought it high time I made my excuses for a trip up the hill to look at the engines.

People who go on package-tour holidays today travel under conditions never dreamed of a quarter of a century ago, in super jets at 600 miles an hour and 30,000ft altitude. Few of them are young. It has taken them a lifetime to make the money to take one of these high-pressure holidays across half the world. Small wonder then that many of them are sick upon arrival and some are a little bemused.

In time one learns to take it all in one's stride. I recall one night when the buzzer sounded its urgent appeal at 3 am—a leopard was on view. One lady appeared all dressed up, including sun hat. She must have thought it a call to abandon ship, supposing The Ark to be sinking.

Then there was the very old gentlemen who was travelling alone. He was understandably tired and grumpy. In the morning we filed out as usual to the vehicles and I counted heads. One guest was missing and, upon returning I found him wandering about—lost. As is often true of the elderly he was so independent that he would allow no help in his packing, not even verbal help. When at last he emerged one of the staff took me by the arm: 'Bwana, he has got his shoes on the wrong feet.' Poor old man. He railed so much at the world in general that nobody plucked up the courage to tell him, and he went back to Nairobi dressed in this peculiar fashion.

Hostesses, as well as Hunters, have to be dedicated, with a ready smile at all times. Even if they are ill themselves they must never show it. The worst night I ever remember was when we had a full house and eight people went down with enteric trouble caught at the last hotel. I doubt if the Hostess managed to get more than a cup of tea of a clear hour of sleep. Four girls shared the duties of hostess during these difficult first two years at The Ark, and I would like here to pay tribute to their devoted work.

The girls were diverse in their appearance and in their countries of origin but united in their dedication to duty. Vena Johansson was the local-born wife of a coffee-estate manager whose father was Swedish and mother English. She was efficient and had a cheerful nature that always made working with her a pleasure. Today she is Housekeeper to the Country Club and The Ark. Anna Bell had been an air hostess. Wife of a British police officer working with the Kenya government, she had been born in India.

Beverly Wood was the wife of a Canadian school teacher. She was the Cinderella of our quartet, destined always to be the Hostess on duty during those rare nights when things went wrong. One such time was during the heavy rains when the big bus and its 32 occupants became hopelessly stuck in the mud halfway up the hill near the Park entrance and the Hunter had to get the passengers up to The Ark in relays, using the small vehicles. It was the day before Christmas Eve and the waiting time was spent singing carols. Beverly was also on duty that night I had to go urgently out of the forest with an injured man and, returning late, saw the litter of almost new-born forest-hogs crossing the road ahead beneath the low-slung belly of the mother.

Doreen Butterworth, the wife of a British teacher, originated from my part of the world, Lancashire. In operating a tourist lodge, one is never certain until the very last moment how many guests there will be. People may fail to arrive. Others may decide to come at the last moment. The Hostess has charge of the rooming list and it is customary to ask what the final figure is. Three Hostesses always gave the exact figure of guests. But not Doreen. If, in a puzzled way, one queried the number, the answer was always the same: 'Wi' thee and me.'

My cabin door at The Ark was never closed at night. I wedged it open with my slippers knowing it gave confidence to any who happened to be sick. One morning, about two-thirty, when I had just dropped off to sleep after a particularly heavy night, I was awakened by a hand on my shoulder. After apologising the guest said he was frantic with headache and could I give him pills. I did everything necessary and assured him it was no trouble at all. In fact I felt genuinely sorry for him. And as I finally turned sleepily on my pillow a voice from the open door said, 'The rhino's back again.'

In those early days before our nightguards were experienced, I always insisted that they awaken me for all animal arrivals they deemed interesting. One night the guard shook me roughly with the magic words: 'Chui (leopard) Bwana.' I had gone to sleep with my face to the wall and, as I jumped up, caught my poor bald pate a fearful crack on the wooden cover over the wall light. Floundering downstairs I called him all the choice names I could think of, but they were nothing to those I used when I found his leopard was nothing more than a hyena. From that night forth he rang the buzzer himself for all leopards.

The nightguard is paid a bonus for either of those two elusive animals, the leopard and the bongo. The sighting has, of course, to be confirmed by the Hunter but the bonus is a wonderful incentive to keeping him awake. Nevertheless nightguards are only human. One night a girl decided she would sit up the whole of the night and so miss nothing. About 3 am she became aware that the nightguard was asleep—and snoring. She shook him but to no avail, so decided it was best to carry on. At 4 am three bongo not only came in but suddenly appeared only a few yards from the bar window. This was too much. She simply raced up-stairs.

I heard the pounding of feet and sat up, opening my eyes in time to see this apparition of loveliness before me. She shook me violently and said: 'Three bongo are in and your nightguard is fast asleep.' Then she fled. When I saw these three beautiful animals close to the building I knew a loud blast on the buzzer would be fatal, so I gave the tiniest of peeps. It was no good. A bedroom door slammed and three bongo bounded away like one animal. And only a lovely girl and myself could say we had seen them. But I wasn't quite sure it hadn't all been a dream. . . .

One of the greatest headaches to all Hunters and Hostesses is the habit some people have of leaving behind articles of value. In the early days a lot accumulated, and many times it was impossible to get them back to the owners, for they were often on a plane to some distant part of the world before the loss was discovered. Eventually, however, we devised a system whereby the whole of the building could be searched before the guests left. Even then things were sometimes lost.

One lady left her passport under her pillow and I had to go post-haste to her next stop, 40 miles away, at Mount Kenya Safari Club. What a look of joy came on her face when she saw it again. Today we fling over all pillows and pull out all drawers in the final search. Yet even now we sometimes find things later—inside the blankets.

One afternoon a lady told me she had lost her gold watch during the short walk from where the vehicles are parked. I went back with her and we searched the ground thoroughly but without success. It had rained and there was a lot of mud. I was not happy and, when I found time later, I went back alone. Eventually I spotted one single glint of gold. It had been trodden 3in below the surface but was quite unharmed and still ticking. After cleaning it I went back, sought her out, took hold of her hand in the dark of the open verandah, and pressed it into her palm. Again, the joyful exclamation was the only reward I needed.

A little girl came with her mother one day. She appeared well under the regulation age of eight but, because she looked so sweet and we were by no means full, we allowed her to go to The Ark. She was keen, so keen that she just would not go to bed but stayed on and on. It was a poor night for game. At last, about 2 am, she could keep her eyes open no longer and her mother trotted her away. At 3 am the elephants came, a big herd with many babies. After sounding the buzzer I went along to their room. The child was so dead asleep that the mother could not rouse her, so I gathered her up in my arms and carried her out into the viewing lounge. There she opened her eyes. Santa Claus and all his reindeer could not have pleased her more than that sight. She watched wide-eyed for a full ten minutes. Then she closed her eyes and, giving a long sigh of contentment, was sound asleep once more.

As I have explained, the windows in the dungeon are merely big slots in the stonework. When guests drop a camera overboard it is quite possible to climb through and retrieve it. But it needs care. One evening the Hostess suddenly remembered that it was a long time since she had seen anything of another young girl so she investigated the dungeon. There was the child, standing on a leather pouffe, leaning out of the open window and trying hard to touch a giant forest-hog grazing just out of reach. Incidentally, during these first three years of The Ark, five different elephants have put their trunks through the windows. That is when the Hunter Guide has indeed to be strict, putting his hand on the little table in the centre of the room, and saying: 'Thus far and no farther.'

Understandably people worry about the care of their money. One Japanese gentleman stuffed all his notes down his sock, forgetting that socks have a habit of working down. Half-way through the night the staff started running to me with currency in their hands. The last I saw of him before going to bed was sitting by the fire trying to add it up to £45. As he knew no English I never did find out if it was correct.

A lady carrying a considerable sum of money thought it would be a good idea to put her wallet under the drawer instead of inside it. Unfortunately, the joiner who built The Ark cabins did not finish the job. He left a space of some 2in at the back and before she realised this her precious wallet had dropped down. The first job was to find tools and dismantle the wooden shelf of which the drawer formed a part. This, however, could not be completed until we first dismantled the bed which held the structure in place. I was by then beginning to wonder if The Ark would remain sea-worthy. Having taken the bed to pieces we obtained a torch and a little mirror and finally located the wallet about 18in down. The only trouble was that nobody had a hand small enough to get through the space.

Aboard The Ark that night was a member of the Russian Embassy staff with his wife and little girl. She knew not a word of English but fortunately her father did. It took a lot of sweets and promises to persuade her to plunge an arm into a hidden space and fish out the wallet.

Another occasion when I had to be resourceful was in those early days when we did not always have a Hostess. A young girl had split her jeans from top to bottom. Now in the Hunter's room there was supposed to be needle and thread, but the thread was used up and had not been replaced. Yet the job was still done—with fuse wire. It is not true that I performed the operation; I merely gave technical advice. A very neat job it was too. We used pliers and cut and twisted it into short lengths. The 'stitching' glittered as she walked.

Heads of State and Royalty have, of course, now visited The Ark but not in the same numbers as Treetops for it will be a long time before we become as well known. It is highly unlikely that we will ever have a young lady embark a Princess and disembark a Queen. Though this was not strictly true of Queen Elizabeth, it is correct that her father died whilst she was actually at Treetops, and that she thus became a queen in all but the actual coronation. Even the most successful advertising agent could not have created more publicity.

My favourite memory is of a shy girl who sat most of the evening in a corner reading, hoping, and largely succeeding, in remaining incognito—Geraldine Chaplin, filmstar and daughter of the great comedian. A newspaper reporter had succeeded in getting into The Ark that night and his identity was not discovered until too late to evict him without a scene. I had to keep him happy but away from her until a few minutes before we left in the morning, when I introduced him discreetly and he got his story.

I was also the Hunter Guide on duty the night Hugh Heffner of *Playboy* fame visited The Ark complete with a bevy of Bunny Girls. If one looks in the visitors' book for that night one can still see where some wit has written in the 'game seen' column: 'Seen after dark—eight bunnies.' I never made up my mind whether it was a compliment or not that the management chose me to be Hunter that night.

The drawbridge at The Ark is raised at night. This is not done just to keep animals out, though, of course, such an eventuality is not impossible. Neither is it for show. The party spirit often runs high amongst young people on holiday and, if too much has been drunk, foolish bets can be made. There was one early morning when a local gentleman actually went for a swim in the pool. He was warned that if he ever did such a thing again then it would be the last National Park he would ever enter.

That is not the only human activity there has been outside The Ark. One man was driving a Land Rover across the Aberdares from the Naivasha side, intending to come out on the road at Treetops. He had with him a lady friend and a child. The vehicle bogged down in a stream about four miles from The Ark when it was nearly dark. By far the most sensible thing would have been to sit and wait for the dawn. (Three years ago much the same thing happened on Mount Kenya. Down the road that gentleman encountered a herd of elephants and was killed.) This man was lucky. He encountered nothing which did not run away and, being local and knowing the forest, he arrived at The Ark about an hour after dark, guided by the lights and partly by the moon.

The drawbridge was, of course, raised and he had to perform a trapeze act to get in, balancing along the catwalk girders. Normally, the nightguard, after raising the drawbridge, bolts the big double doors on the inside. That particular night he forgot, and so the stranger gained admittance. He was muddy, wet, tired and hungry. We lent him a driver, a vehicle rope and a torch. After some refreshment they both left and the vehicle was duly pulled out.

Another uninvited guest came to The Ark, and in fact he has now been three times. The first two I was not on duty but the last time he simply walked out of the bushes in full view. He is an African from a village not many miles away, a simpleton who just cannot appreciate the fact that there is anything wrong. He is not a poacher and carries only a little stick like a swagger cane. He calls at The Ark, asking for a cup of tea or other such simple requirement. We bundle him down to the police and eventually he goes inside for a little spell. He is quite harmless and should go to a home, but has no real home to go to. Where it will end I just don't know. Apparently the last time he came, a great herd of elephants filled the glade and, like that old buffalo bull, he just walked through them. Being so simple he would not experience fear and the elephants possibly sensed this.

There is no question that the Aberdare National Park is a tremendous asset to Kenya and a means of saving many thousands of animals from ultimate destruction through the revenue derived from places like The Ark. Nevertheless it would be quite wrong to think that this has been achieved without heartbreak and suffering. I would like here to pay homage to a class of people whose numbers are now declining fast, and I would like my readers to remember them too. They are the very old Africans who live around the perimeter of this huge mountain. Possibly they were born within its boundaries. Certainly they spent their youth wandering through its forests. They hunted the animals and they ate the fruits of the trees. Today they are left with only their memories.

At one time I used a coding system at The Ark to announce on the buzzer what species of animal had arrived. Then we had a honeymoon couple to stay. At 3 am when the buzzer sounded they could not tell how many dots or dashes there had been. They said I was to blame for the 'biggest quarrel of their married life'. So the coding system was abolished. Nevertheless it is quite easy to put a great degree of urgency in the sound of the peeps. This is still done when leopards appear. Unless a guest moves quickly there is a fair chance that he will miss seeing them —baiting with meat is not allowed in a National Park.

One night, about 10 pm, I sounded the buzzer to summon guests quickly because a leopard was in front of the viewing lounge. Two young ladies were caught out in the showers. Looking like two blue mummies they waddled into the lounge swathed in every bathtowel they could find. They left a row of wet footprints across the carpet. But they saw the leopard.

A lot of humorous remarks are made at The Ark, either subconsciously or because the person has no knowledge whatever of game. Consider these priceless comments, mostly heard in the darkness of the viewing lounge.

One night a lady was staring long and earnestly into an empty glade. Suddenly she looked up and said: 'Now I know the difference between a male and female bush.' I'm still wondering what she meant.

One man had been looking at two of the rarely seen, beautiful bongo, quite close to the building for a full twenty minutes. Suddenly he turned to me, saying: 'Say, when are the big cats coming in?'

One woman to another: 'You know there are two kinds of hippopotamuses, one that lives in water and one that lives on the land. The one that they have here is the one that lives on the land.'

A black rhino was walking into the glade one night and a lady guest said: 'There's a white rhino coming in.' 'That isn't a white rhino' came an answer out of the darkness. 'Well, if it isn't white it's beige.'

Bemoaning the fact that she did not hear the buzzer and so see the two leopards one lady said: 'Well, I did take my sleeping pills as usual.'

A little girl who had been listening to the conversation about the giant forest-hogs asked: 'Did *you* see the giant hedgehogs, Mummy?'

A dear old lady was talking to her friend: 'What did you say those animals were?' 'Wart-hogs' was the reply. 'Oh, I thought you said war dogs.'

Humorous comments at The Ark were not confined to the viewing lounge. From the powder room one night when the buzzer was sounded a lady was reported to have asked: 'What have I done wrong now?'

The comments of the lady who sat down on her bed just after the staff had placed a hot-water bottle in it, and who thought that the genet cat had beaten her to it are, unfortunately, not to be repeated.

Even away out at the viewpoint, the name given to the place where The Ark is first seen, has not been without its humour. 'That is The Ark', announced the Hostess once. 'Look, Mary,' came a voice, 'the lady says there's a yak.'

A little boy passing the Hunter's room and seeing the rifle standing in a corner remarked: 'Daddy, I could have brought my airgun after all.'

One very noisy lady had a lot to say, and the Hostess warned her a number of times. A big bull elephant came on to the salt in front of the glassed-in viewing lounge and the buzzer was sounded. The noisy lady came tripping along with her husband tagging behind. A moment later she saw the elephant and fell absolutely silent. As the long-suffering husband came past the

Hostess he smiled and said: 'If it only takes an elephant to make her quiet then I'll buy a couple from you.'

A big herd of elephants once stood in front of The Ark with a huge bull in their midst. A dear old lady sitting with her back to the scene said to the Hostess: 'How do you tell which are boys and which are girls?' Before the Hostess could think of a suitable answer the bull decided to demonstrate to the whole world that he at least was not a girl. Blissfully unaware of this, the dear old lady repeated her question, to the uncontrollable merriment of all assembled. The Hostess fled. As the comment was voiced later, that big bull was well endowed.

One night a lady came into the darkened viewing lounge. There were six buffalo standing placidly at the waterside. From some angles they were reflected in the glass of the far side of the room. Not looking at the people sitting quietly there she spotted the reflection and screamed: 'The elephants are coming', and, before she could be stopped, ran back and roused the whole building.

Some of the moths at The Ark are big. A gentleman had been watching the genet pounce on one in fairly long grass, and it took a little while to eat, the wings falling on each side of the genet's mouth. Later he was heard describing the event to a friend. But the story went something like this: 'I saw a mongoose catch a snake and eat it. There was such a big fight.'

Two very important ladies were once sent from a well-known tourist company. As we travelled in the Land Rover they told me that they didn't care if they saw no other animals at all as long as they saw a leopard. About tea-time a leopard came out of the bushes and was watched for quite a time by the guests. I didn't think it possible that anybody had missed seeing them, but it transpired that these two had gone to lie down and so were too late.

I had told them always to look out of their cabin window first should the buzzer be sounded at night. About 3 am two hyenas wandered into the glade and, as usual, I sounded 'a lousy pip for a lousy hyena'. These two it seems shot out of bed, looked out of the window, and sat entranced. Next morning I heard them telling a large audience how they had heard the buzzer in the night and watched two leopards walk right across the glade. Nobody else it appeared had bothered to get up for that 'lousy little pip'. Or at least they never said anything. There are times when a Hunter must keep silent and that was one.

The Ark is a living ship and happily such incidents will go on and on. The concept of a viewing lodge deep in the forest, breaking new ground in the field of game viewing, has proved itself over three highly successful years. For my own part I can only end this account of those years with the pensive question put to me by a New York typist after a particularly wonderful night.

'What is it like working in paradise?'

The Ark Is Built

High on a lonely mountain side,
By a pool, in a grassy glade,
Nestling in forests deep and wide,
An Ark by man has been made.

An Ark by man has been born,
In forests belonging to God.
Where only His beasts have worn
Those trails we see searing the sod.

No man-made machine has defiled this land,
'Tis the same that Dinosaurs trod.
'Tis the same that Reptiles walked upon,
In these forests belonging to God.

The Bongo are drinking this pool tonight,
Ndongoro the little men called him on sight,
With huge twisted horns and stripes gleaming white,
The ghosts of the forest, ever shunning the light.

How many dark-skinned hunters of old
Have squatted out there, where this little glade narrows?
How many skin-clad hunters bold
Sat with gut-strung bows and eagle-winged arrows?

In those peaty depths
How many bones lie hidden?
How many broken arrows and spears
Tell a silent story of hopes and fears?

How many times have the pachyderms killed
In their fight with a primitive foe?
How many times has a brave heart been stilled
Down by the water below?

Now these battles are over between beast and man,
And surely the wild has won.
No longer they need to climb up in an Ark,
There is room for us all in the sun.

R. J. Prickett

Index